The Price

When Bookkeeping Means Bookcooking

The Price

When Bookkeeping Means Bookcooking

Nantoo Banerjee

frontpage

frontpage

www.frontpagepublications.com

First published 2011

Frontpage Publications Limited
5 Percy Street, London W1T 1DG, United Kingdom

Frontpage
Level 6, Constantia
11 Dr U N Brahmachari Sarani, Kolkata 700017, India

ISBN: 978 93 810430 3 5

Printed in India
By Sadhana Press Private Limited
76 B B Ganguly Street, Kolkata 700012, India

Typeset by Compuset International
85 Park Street, Kolkata 700016, India

Contents

To my parents

Acknowledgements

This story on the price of bookcooking took almost two years to materialise mainly because of the difficulties in terms of logistics, distances involved and in accessing the concerned people and institutions for information and comment. Although the epicentre of the crime was Hyderabad in Andhra Pradesh, agencies involved in investigation were spread across Mumbai, Hyderabad, Delhi, Bangalore and New York.

While industry has been traditionally allergic to self-criticism, regulators normally shy away from providing tangible information on fraud fearing it may expose their own laxity in the process of detecting or probing a crime. Yet, a number of well-meaning persons concerned about growing accounting frauds and the poor state of corporate governance were very helpful and came forward to help build the story. I express my sincere gratitude to all of them, including those who requested anonymity. But for their help this story would never have been complete.

Vinod Rai, the Comptroller and Auditor General of India, was extremely generous in helping me understand the issue of auditor-client alliance and the possible safeguards against it, the practice of auditing government and public sector accounts, the need for conducting periodical special audits and peer reviews.

D Bandyopadhyay, Secretary in the Department of Corporate Affairs, Government of India, had very kindly spoken about the changes the Draft Companies' Bill sought to incorporate ensuring better corporate governance and greater reliability of audited corporate accounts. A number of senior officials in the departments connected with the preparation of the draft bill, including Joint Secretary Avinash K Srivastava, director and legal advisor, participated separately in a matter-of-fact discussion on accounting fraud and how the provisions in the proposed Companies Act sought to address the issue.

Top industry professionals such as former E&Y chairman Amal C Chakrabortti, former ICAI president Ved Jain, eminent chartered accountant Samir Ganguly, parliamentarian and steering committee member Gurudas Dasgupta, business-personality Umang Kejriwal, and retired IRS officer Abhijit Bhattacharyya had shared their views on the issue without prejudice. I am grateful to all of them for enrichment of my knowledge.

Lastly, I will fail in my duty if I do not express my deep appreciation for some close associates of Ramalinga Raju who too shared their points of view in the matter and spoke at length about the IT industry's recruitment, billing and accounting practices. Probity prevents me from naming those professionals and valiant executives, who admitted that they were aware of the existence of 'surplus' employees in the Satyam pay roll but did not know if that was to inflate the billing. They claimed they had no knowledge of the accounting fraud at Satyam until Raju himself confessed to it.

NANTOO BANERJEE
January 2011

Introduction

How reliable and trustworthy are corporate books of accounts? Why are public companies, banks and financial institutions going bankrupt without prior and proper knowledge of shareholders and creditors? Why does only the top management of a corporation or an institution know the true financial health of the organisation? Aren't the auditors too – internal and external – supposed to know or find out and report the true financial picture of the organisation for the benefit of stakeholders?

The statutory obligation of fair reporting and analysing of an organisation's books of accounts by an external auditor is to all shareholders and not to the top management alone. How often do auditors deviate from this noble role under pressure from management?

Today accounting professionals, performing audit functions, are fully equipped to detect any wrong financial engineering and malpractice by a corporate or institutional management. The knowledge is available. The technology is available. Yet, why do auditors of many wrong-doing business organisations shy away from reporting the truth to stakeholders in time or before it is too late?

The power of auditors has been lately demonstrated by India's largest statutory auditor, the Comptroller & Auditor General of India, a constitutional body, exposing the irregularities in the 2G spectrum allotment deals with private telecom companies, robbing the exchequer revenues up to Rs 1,76,000 crores (US$ 39 billion), which nearly rocked the country's Congress-led multi-party coalition government, resulting in the exit of the telecommunications minister Andimuthu Raja and inviting Supreme Court's veiled stricture against Prime Minister Manmohan Singh of 'inaction'.

These government auditors worked fearlessly in the interest of the nation and not to please the powers to be. Honesty and integrity of audit professionals and their views, as expressed in audit reports, provide essential ingredients to good governance. When bookkeeping turns into book-cooking, the price the society pays is naturally very heavy.

India has already been paying a heavy price on account of illegal transfer of funds by corporates and individuals, including politicians, bureaucrats, businessmen and their agents, ever since Independence. A painstaking study by Global Financial Integrity (GFI), a US-based non-profit research body, on 'The Drivers and Dynamics of Illicit Financial Flows from India:1948-2008' concluded that India was drained of US$ 462 billion during this period, although much of it took place after the government's economic reforms process in 1991-92. According to Dev Kar, economist and the author of the GFI report, "this is the most comprehensive study on illicit financial flows from India ever attempted". Kar stands by the study. On the other hand, the Bharatiya Janata Party, the country's second largest national party after Congress, claims that the amount of illegal funds stashed abroad would be to the tune of US$ 1.4 trillion.

The illegal transfers referred to are mostly tax-evaded funds or 'unaccounted' money, generated mainly by cooking up books of accounts, income and expenditure statements, shady export-import deals, using routes such as unrecorded wire transfers, 'hawala' transactions or currency swaps, under-invoicing and over-invoicing of export and import, the use of couriers and cross-border currency smuggling.

Although, it is now fashionable to talk about business ethics and corporate governance in private and public forums, in reality, good governance is becoming increasingly difficult to come by. Good governance is like trying to locate a good, honest, wise and efficient politician, a rare occurrence.

The economic melt-down across the globe is a direct fall-out of some unethical, reckless business practices indulged in by some of the world's top investment bankers, corporate behemoths, financial audit firms and credit rating agencies, in total disregard of the codes of corporate governance as they exist in many parts of the world. Corporate governance is all about following good business ethics and good management practices for the benefit of shareholders in general and the society at large. Mahatma Gandhi called it business trusteeship. The need for strict compliance of corporate governance codes is, once again, drawing global attention as an increasing number of greedy errant corporate head honchos on get-rich-quick errands are trying to bring down national governments and the global economy to their knees in order to satiate their never ending lust for money.

Effective compliance, however, is easier said than done. Human greed is too strong to be regulated easily even by an all-powerful State as has been proved time and again. Some greedy corporate bosses are like efficient physicians who become psychopathic killers, with no regard for law or life.

Ironically, the maximum violation of corporate governance codes is taking place in the United States, which boasts of the presence of the world's most stringent corporate governance laws, especially after the enactment of Sarbanes-Oxley Act of 2002.

The enactment of the Sarbanes-Oxley law by the US federal government followed the collapse of a number of large US firms in 2001 such as Enron Corporation, WorldCom, America On-Line, Arthur Andersen, Adelphia, Global Crossing, Fannie Mae, Freddie Mac and Peregrine Systems. The Act is also known as the Public Company Accounting Reform and Investor Protection Law, 2002. Events of mid-2008 once again proved how helpless such laws could become in the face of insatiable corporate greed as illustrated by the actions of some of the highest earning board members of some of the world's most valuable public corporations as also by the inaction of those gullible and easily-corruptible 'independent' directors decorating those boardrooms.

The track record of corporate governance in the world's third largest economy, Japan, too has been as bad and is much criticised in the US and the United Kingdom without much impact on Japanese corporates. Dai-Ichi Kangyo of Japan, one of the world's largest and most solvent commercial banks till the early 1980s, was brought down by its greedy management under the pressure of huge sticky loans, prompting a present US-style financial rescue act by the Japanese government in those days. The hiring of musclemen by corporate management to silence the dissenting voices of minority shareholders at annual general meetings is alleged be a common practice in Japan, showcasing a keidenran management tradition that discouraged competition among large Japanese enterprises and job hopping by employees for better opportunity, personal development, higher remuneration and faster growth.

The concept of corporate governance as preached in the western world is rather new in India. In the 1970s and 1980s, India's banking sector was saddled with huge bad corporate sector debts totalling some Rs 2-3 lakh crores. However, industrial sickness seldom affected the promoters and their lifestyle. Funds were regularly siphoned out from their enterprises by corporate promoters in the name of diversification. Inter-connected companies provided financial security to these promoter-managers. High debt equity ratio allowed to industrial promoters by the government in the 1970s and 1980s helped business houses run public companies with holdings as low as 5-10 per cent of the paid-up capital. Many of these enterprises became sick inflicting heavy financial blows on State-owned financial institutions such as the Industrial Development Bank of India and Industrial Finance Corporation of India. The erring promoter-managers went scot-free. Conversion of corporate capital into family assets was common. Corporate audit reports rarely reflected a true and fair view of the books of accounts of these companies. As a result, shareholders and creditors of the companies suffered enormous losses.

The massive financial fraud at Satyam Computers, India's fourth largest software company until 2008, should not be mistaken as an isolated case. The Satyam promoters wanted to convert a huge chunk of the company's corporate wealth into their private family asset. It failed to do so in the face of strong protests from institutional shareholders. No one could imagine that Satyam Computers' phoenix-like rise would suddenly receive such a jolt. Thanks to the foolishness – or, blame it to an uncontrolled greed – of its founder-chairman, B Ramalinga Raju, the company got itself into a big mess. A timely rescue act by Mumbai's Mahindra & Mahindra group saved the company and majority of its employees. Raju's own holding in Satyam was only 8.5 per cent. Institutional shareholders controlled over 51 per cent.

A formal probe by the Securities and Exchange Board of India (SEBI), the market watchdog, into the company's corporate governance failure and other related issues, including possible insider trading by Satyam promoters, directors and Raju's family members over the years, and Satyam's Nagarjuna Finance link may expose a can of worms about the way the promoters conducted the affairs of the public company. In trying to transfer a huge amount of cash, totalling some US$ 1.6 billion, from Satyam in favour of the chairman's sons in exchange of their two realty and infrastructure firms, Raju lost the confidence of his company's majority shareholders and control over Satyam.

According to law, every joint stock company in India is required to include its corporate governance compliance statement in its annual report. But much of it is hog wash. The SEBI committee on corporate governance defines corporate governance as "the acceptance by the management of the inalienable rights of shareholders as true owners of the corporation". The SEBI report emphasises on "commitment to values and ethical standards" and "making a distinction between personal and corporate funds in the management of a company". But, does anyone really give any credence to these lofty SEBI guidelines? Does SEBI itself believe in them and act tough with the violators?

Assets of public corporations in India are split at will by fighting family members of the promoters' clan among themselves. Are these ethical business standards? Do these promoters behave as 'trustees on behalf of the shareholders'? These are tricky questions. Neither SEBI, nor corporate management, appears to be truly concerned about such issues.

Even in highly professional business environments such as in the US, the UK, France, Germany, Italy and Spain, corporate governance seems to receive lip service. Unholy relationships between corporate CEOs and boards of directors – including the so-called independent directors – enabling fat fees, commissions and stock options (not infrequently backdated) often makes a mockery of corporate governance. Independence of statutory auditors is often a myth as these audit firms are becoming increasingly dependent on high-earning non-audit consultancy services they provide to their clients, directly or indirectly. Even large institutional shareholders gloss over many wrong doings of corporate managements as long as profits, dividends and share prices maintain their uptrend.

Transparency, accountability and management integrity in business deals and financial transactions of a company, hallmarks of good corporate governance, were not certainly exercised in the recently failed US, UK and European investment banks and industrial enterprises. If the existence of stringent corporate governance laws requiring setting up of 'public company accounting oversight boards', financial disclosure of 'off-balance sheet transactions', signing of corporate tax returns by CEOs, corporate and criminal fraud accountability and heavy penalty for 'white collar crimes' have failed to deter western corporate management from acting like a bunch of irresponsible financial crooks, there is little hope for ethical business standards anywhere in the world. It will require a complete change in the mindset of corporate management, putting business ethics before personal gain and corporate profit to make the principle of corporate governance work.

When Price Waterhouse returned the mandate to the board of the late M R Chhabria-controlled Dunlop India Limited as one of its two statutory auditors in the early 1990s, Dunlop's ordinary shareholders knew little about the true and fair picture of the company's financial health and its future despite certain qualifications made by the auditors and the contingent liability on the company. The automotive and aero-tyre giant, once the country's largest, had even declared dividend from its non-existent surplus. The auditors' report of the annual accounts was qualified but there was nothing to indicate the massive siphoning out of funds by the company's promoters and the possibility of the company's net worth getting eroded to be in the negative in the very next year. Dunlop headed for closure. NRI Chhabria was not bothered. The other statutory auditor, Lodha & Co, was willing to continue giving a confusing signal to shareholders and creditors. Dunlop's Dubai-based promoters managed to have their way.

Dunlop's story was not very different from corporate giants and banks such as GKW, Metal Box, GEC of India, Shaw Wallace and Hyderabad-based Global Trust Bank, which sank under the heavy burden of non-performing assets or bad debts. They collapsed almost overnight to the shock and dismay of their innocent, ignorant investors who trusted the annual reports and audited accounts of these high-profile business organisations. The massive siphoning out of funds from packaging giant Metal Box by its management through an unrelated Satyam-Maytas style diversification into a bearing-manufacturing project using wrongly-invoiced imported capital goods escaped the scrutiny of the company's statutory auditors and bankers. The Metal Box public issue of bonds was strongly recommended by its merchant bankers. The company collapsed soon after installing the ball-bearing project. The management of these once mega-multinational companies enjoyed such 'cosy' relations with their ever obliging statutory auditors and bankers that the ordinary shareholders remained in the dark about the true financial health of their companies until it was too late.

The financial mismanagement in those companies in the 1980s and 1990s was, however, much less grievous than that in Satyam Computers Services, the globally operating Indian software company, whose disgraced founder-chairman B Ramalinga Raju surprised the corporate world on 7 January 2009 with a voluntary disclosure of financial fraud that left its statutory auditors, bankers, credit rating and equity grading agencies totally red-faced. Raju admitted to committing the biggest ever financial fraud in India's corporate history, inflicting a nearly Rs 7,000-

crore hole in Satyam's books of accounts. The techniques used to fudge Satyam's books of accounts did not involve any highly intricate 'financial engineering' which should have escaped the eyes of the company's statutory auditors, credit rating agencies, bankers and financial analysts. The methods adopted for the window dressing of Satyam's financial accounts were inflating the company's sales income and profits, overstating the company's cash and reserves and understating its liabilities. The application of these fraudulent accounting practices is more or less common with all rogue companies and their management, which professional auditors, credit rating agencies, banks and financial analysts are trained to detect and question.

It is hard to believe that the auditors at Price Waterhouse Coopers (PwC), the world's largest financial audit firm, did not know that their client, the US-listed Satyam Computers, was following fraudulent accounting practices for years with ruthless efficiency. It is equally surprising that credit rating agencies innocently glossed over the accounting malpractices year after year. It is also shocking that Satyam's shrewd bankers did not care to know or notice where the Indian software major was parking its huge 'surplus' cash, around Rs 5,300 crores (US$ 1.3 billion), that was shown in the company's books of accounts. An accounting fraud of this magnitude could not have been perpetuated over a period of time without complicity as well as professional laxity on the part of the internal and external inspection agencies. The roles of the company's board level audit committee and its independent directors associated with it cannot be ignored in such a case of well-organised accounting forgery.

The financial fraud at Satyam Computers is reminiscent of accounts jugglery and stock price manipulation by Enron in the US. Enron's auditors, Arthur Andersen, were so condemned for their alleged complicity with the financial crime that they got disintegrated even before the federal regulatory agencies and the court finished with their proceedings against the US energy giant.

It is most unlikely that PwC or its local associate member in India will suffer a similar ignominy and go bust following its failure to live up to the trust of Satyam shareholders, including financial institutions, without whose approval the company could not have appointed the firm as its statutory auditors. The latter have also badly let down the company's 53,000 employees, many of whom may have taken stock options as part of their remuneration package and were on the verge of losing their jobs. It is also unlikely that the Institute of Chartered Accountants of India (ICAI), the self regulatory body of the practicing chartered accountants, will act tough with PwC for its failure to uphold the global and local accounting standards. Many feel that ICAI has not been generally very tough on 'big brothers' in the business.

Raju and his accomplices in the financial crime may also be accused of heavy insider trading in Satyam shares, the prices of which were highly rigged on the basis of the glossy picture the company projected in its balance sheets and annual reports. They might have indulged in reckless insider trading reaping huge profits by selling junk shares at high prices to ignorant investors who trusted the company's statements. Even though he denies the charge, this may explain why Raju, who knew the real worth of Satyam shares, brought down his own holding in the company to very low levels. Raju cannot get away with his 'honest' admission that he authorised the juggling of Satyam accounts in the interest of the company and its future business. He and his men made a mockery of corporate governance at Satyam Computers. The trustworthiness of Raju's 'voluntary disclosure' of the company's highly imaginative bookkeeping is also questioned by many. Perhaps Raju was up to a bigger financial conspiracy to remove large amounts of cash from the company. It is likely that the 'non-existent' cash story was a lie. Cash did exist. Raju & Co may have illegally removed them over a period of time. No one knows. There are no clear answers to such questions as yet.

Unfortunately, regulatory agencies and the government failed to act fast and take exemplary action against the promoters and auditors. Why were the independent directors allowed to walk free? ICAI, on its part, must quiz the concerned Price Waterhouse auditors to find how they overlooked the massive overstatement of the company's assets over the years, amounting to nearly Rs 7,000 crores mostly in cash and bank balance, take cautionary action against the erring auditors and make their modus operandi public.

Satyam's should have been treated as a strong test case by all concerned regulatory bodies, including SEBI, the government's department of company affairs, registrar of companies and enforcement directorate and the RBI to ensure strict compliance of corporate governance in public business and strongly restore local as well as global investors' confidence in India Inc.

The suggestion of peer review of audited accounts of select blue chip companies by market regulator SEBI has sent shivers down the spine of many large listed corporations. The securities watchdog is seriously considering a cross-check of the annual audited numbers of high-profile public companies of the Bombay stock exchange's sensitive 30-share index, SENSEX, or the National stock exchange's 50-share NIFTY. Some of them are trying their best to get the SEBI move scuttled. Not surprisingly, even ICAI is somewhat cagey about the proposed peer review of a company's books of accounts. Influential members of ICAI would instead prefer periodical rotation of statutory auditors by public companies and the strengthening of the internal audit system.

By suggesting a peer review of an audited account, SEBI wants to ensure that companies do not cook up their books of accounts at will. Although the cooking of accounts may not be a common practice among large corporate entities in India, not all balance sheets and annual reports of companies, banks and financial institutions reveal all their vital numbers. Business organisations are known to window-dress their books of accounts to suit stakeholder communication needs. The Satyam computers' case of bookkeeping malpractices only adds a new dimension to the old practice, both in degree and kind.

The methodologies commonly adopted for fudging accounts include hiding profits and losses, overstatement of incomes and profits, understatement of taxable income, under-realisation from sale of assets, misrepresentation of commissions, distribution costs and other post-manufacturing expenses, inflated input costs, overpriced acquisitions, misuse of business promotion fund for personal gains, siphoning of funds through a number of means such as keeping rosters of 'ghost' employees and kickbacks from unnecessary purchases, corporate donations, charities, corporate social responsibility programmes and advertising spends.

Many companies belonging to both the private and public sectors had, in the past, faced official investigations into and special audits of books of accounts. The prominent among them were STC, MMTC and ITC Limited. What SEBI has proposed for large listed companies has long been carried out in public sector undertakings (PSUs) by the Comptroller and Auditor General of India (CAG). SEBI's latest suggestion is the first bold move by the market regulator against large and powerful listed companies in its nearly two-decade-old existence.

Industry feels SEBI's suggestion is unfair and uncalled for as it will only create confusion and delay the announcement of financial results of a company to the detriment of the interest of investors, other stakeholders and the business itself. It may have a negative bearing on stock prices. It is argued that one cuckoo does not make a summer – Satyam Computers' fudging of accounts is a stray case, it should not necessarily make the management of all large public companies suspect of financial conspiracy. By ordering peer reviews of corporate audited accounts, SEBI will overstep its job as a market regulator and usurp the function of a self-appointed inspector or controller of public corporate accounts.

Considering the political and financial clout these companies enjoy, SEBI may be forced to strike peace with the industry and go for softer options, if at all. Too many vested interests are preventing SEBI from performing its proclaimed function as a strong and effective market regulator on the lines of USA's Securities & Exchange Commission (SEC), on which it was supposed to have been originally modelled.

Under the circumstances, the clamour for good corporate governance is unlikely to yield desired results soon. It is not going to be easy to build an effective safeguard against corrupt corporate financial practices without involving multiple agencies – not the audit community alone – and creating strong deterrents. If creation of such safeguards is considered less easy even in developed countries, it is going to be even more difficult in India where cases of financial fraud, especially by large corporations involving bureaucrats, politicians, banks and independent regulatory agencies, are rarely treated as a major crime and attract exemplary punishment.

India's growth story has two parts, one accounted and the other unaccounted. No one can authoritatively claim which of the two parts is bigger. This book merely deals with issues involving only one part of corporate financial corruption that is 'bookcooking' in connivance with auditors, bankers, credit rating agencies and the government. All of them have a deeply embedded role in the financial system. It is based on a specific accounting fraud case of a public company, Satyam Computers, a stock exchange listed giant both in India and the US. Naturally, there are several global connects and references. It is a journalist's account of a developing local story with global implications since both Satyam computers and its eminent auditors operated internationally.

CHAPTER I

The Complaint

Funny are the ways of India's official treatment of financial crime and corruption. Even a public confession of one's act of crime does not seem to be enough to take cognisance of the crime and book the self-proclaimed offender by law enforcement agencies. This is despite the existence of a plethora of laws and sections under the Indian Penal Code to punish such culprits. The law of the land and its enforcement agencies are very particular about procedural perfection before they make the first move even if that means an awful waste of precious time giving an opportunity to the offender to tamper with evidences.

This explains why the public confession of a US$ 1.45-billion (Rs 7,000 crores @ Rs 48/US$ 1 as of January 2009) financial offence committed by B Ramalinga Raju, the then Chairman of the Indian multinational information technology corporation Satyam Computers, was not good enough a reason for law enforcement agencies to act swiftly in booking Raju, other board members and the company's statutory auditors, Price Waterhouse, but for whose possible collusion the country's biggest ever corporate financial fraud was seemingly impossible.

All the offices and establishments of Satyam Computers and key Raju family companies and also residences and bank accounts of the concerned top people, including audit partners, should have been simultaneously raided without delay. The stock market watchdog,

Securities and Exchange Board of India (SEBI), the Institute of Chartered Accountants of India (ICAI), Serious Frauds Office of the government were not pro-active enough to start *suo moto* investigation with the urgency the country's biggest ever financial and accounting fraud deserved.

SEBI should have smelt the fraud well in advance after the company sought to make a massive fund diversion from Satyam to acquire two of Ramalinga Raju's family-promoted firms, which had to be abandoned after the Satyam Computers board received flak from the company's institutional shareholders. The forced derailment of the company's two proposed acquisitions for about US$ 1.6 billion, which were cleared by the board of directors of Satyam Computers, including the so-called independent members, exposed the skeletons in its cupboards and compelled Raju to confess to financial frauds of such a large magnitude.

SEBI should have tried to find out the possible nature of financial irregularities in the company as soon as its institutional shareholders threatened to take legal action against the Satyam board. The law enforcement agencies debated on procedural matters for 48 hours (or, were they waiting for clearance from their political masters?) before acting on a formal police complaint against the company and its auditors for breach of trust before arresting Ramalinga Raju. The two Price Waterhouse partners were arrested more than two weeks after the confession to the crime by the company's chairman on 7 January 2009 and 14 days after a police complaint lodged by an aggrieved woman shareholder.

It was an ordinary looking complaint by a retired woman, Leena Mangat, with the Hyderabad branch of the Crime Investigation Department (CID) of Andhra Pradesh Police on 9 January 2009, against the auditors and the key executive management team of Satyam Computers Services Limited alleging severe financial irregularities in the company's books of accounts. Ironically, this – and not Raju's confession to crime – led to a full-scale investigation into the affairs of Satyam Computers first by the CID of Andhra Pradesh and then by the more powerful Central Bureau of Investigation (CBI) of the Government of India. Other investigations into the crime by agencies such as Serious Frauds Office of the Union Government, Institute of Chartered Accountants of India, Securities and Exchange Board of India and Enforcement Directorate of the Union Finance ministry followed.

Leena Mangat said that she had invested part of her retirement benefits in Satyam Computers shares about four years back on the basis of the company's performance as represented in and reflected through the balance sheet. She bought the shares at a high premium hoping that the price would appreciate further which it did over the next few years on the strength of the company's 'strong' financial performance as shown in the books of accounts, auditors' report, chairman's statement, all projecting a bullish future for Satyam shares. To her horror, the price of Satyam shares suddenly nosedived as the news of Satyam Computers' cooked-up accounts spread like wild fire across the markets. The stock market reacted fast. The share price dropped by over 80 per cent within hours of B Ramalinga Raju's confession to fraud before the company's board of directors.

Like Leena Mangat, thousands of Satyam's small ordinary shareholders were totally at a loss with the rapid fall of the share price in the market as the company's certified and audited accounts and balance sheet turned bogus. Satyam's financials and the bottom line suddenly turned from 'black' to 'deep red'. For investors, it was a gruesome murder in broad day light. The share price dropped from Rs 500 to Rs 35 each. And, there were few takers even at such a low price. The Satyam counter was witnessing a bloodbath that pulled down the company's net asset value by hundreds of millions of rupees. The ordinary investors still failed to understand what was happening as they had full trust in the capability of Price Waterhouse, a member of PricewaterhouseCoopers (PwC), the world's largest audit firm, and its 'unimpeachable' accounting standards.

Accounts must disclose arithmetical accuracy. Who would know this better than the British-American multinational audit firm, PwC? It is the 'true and fair view' of the statutory auditors, who sign and certify the accounts, that ultimately stamps the shareholders' trust on these accounts. There ought to be something basically wrong somewhere with regard to Satyam accounts, many thought. Leena Mangat wanted a thorough investigation into the books of accounts by the CID. But, the public outcry against the Satyam management, its mercurial promoter-chairman B Ramalinga Raju, who had earlier made a stunning public confession of the cooking-up of the company's books of accounts, strong dissent from the powerful foreign and local institutional investors and political pressure forced the union government to press CBI to investigate into India's biggest ever accounting fraud.

CBI is the highest crime and corruption investigating agency of the Indian government designed on the lines of Federal Bureau of Investigation (FBI) of the United States of America (minus the authority of conducting undercover operations) and Scotland Yard of the United Kingdom. What came out of the CBI probe, as listed in the CBI charge sheet, was a mind-boggling bookkeeping fraud and the projection of an amazing laxity and inexplicable carelessness on the part of the company's statutory auditors, Price Waterhouse, in inspecting the company's statement of accounts for several years in succession. CBI sleuths, apparently convinced about the complicity, if not conspiracy, of two Price partners, had them arrested and put behind the bars, several days after the arrest of the company's chairman, B Ramalinga Raju.

The US$ 2-billion Satyam Computers was India's fourth largest information technology (IT) and software services firm until 2008, boasting of several Fortune 500 companies as its clients. The company is listed with a number of stock exchanges in India as also with the New York Stock Exchange (NYSE). PwC is the world's largest financial audit firm represented in India by the member firm, Price Waterhouse. Few shareholders would suspect Price Waterhouse's complicity in Satyam Computers' systematic accounting fraud of such a magnitude.

The arrest of 60-year-old Subramani Gopalkrishnan, a chartered accountant (CA) and the partner-in-charge of Price Waterhouse's

Hyderabad operations, and 48-year-old Talluri Srinivas, also a chartered accountant and a Price Waterhouse partner, both on 23 January 2009, was the talk of the town and remained the biggest talking point ever among auditors and accounting professionals across the country. Not many were surprised about the sheepish way PwC's apex body in India responded to the CBI action against its partners. The audit firm did not stand firmly by its partners or sought their release from custody. At the time of CBI's presentation of final charge sheet and report on the accounting fraud at Satyam on 7 April 2009, the two Price Waterhouse partners were still cooling their heels under judicial custody in Hyderabad along with clients, B Ramalinga Raju and his brother and erstwhile Satyam Computers managing director B Rama Raju, among others. In fact, they spent the whole of 2009 and beyond under judicial custody.

Leena Mangat said in her complaint (Crime No. 2/2009) with the state CID police in Hyderabad that she invested her retirement benefits to buy 100 shares of Satyam Computers for a total sum of Rs 19,000 about four years back and 'due to the fudging of the company accounts and manipulation of records showing incorrect, inflated balance sheets by the chairman, MD and other directors of the company which were certified by the auditors, the value of the shares suddenly dropped causing huge financial loss to her'. The price of Satyam shares had briefly gone up to over Rs 700 each before it crashed. In his confessional letter to the board of directors of Satyam Computers on 7 January 2009, B Ramalinga Raju had stated that the company's balance sheet for the quarter ended on 30 September 2008, carried non-existent cash and bank balances to the tune of Rs 5,040 crores (US$ 1.1 billion). It was too big a shock to be absorbed by any stock market.

The auditors had let down the shareholders, who had been appointing them year after year, having full trust in the professional competence of the associate of the world's leading audit firm. The shareholders had also shown great magnanimity in raising the audit fees of Price Waterhouse year after year as proposed by the company's board in notice to shareholders before annual general meetings of Satyam Computers. Satyam shareholders were not an ignorant lot. Investors included those in the USA, local and global mutual funds operators, local and foreign financial institutions, companies and public trusts, high net-worth individuals and a large section of educated small individual investors having fairly good knowledge about the IT industry, the worth of technology stocks and the market. They trusted Satyam Computers' balance sheets and the company's profit and loss account because they had full faith in the efficiency and integrity of its statutory auditors, Price Waterhouse.

In fact, PwC is a much bigger brand than Satyam Computers. The company probably could not have got it listed in the New York Stock Exchange (NYSE) if it did not engage the services of a global audit firm of such repute to certify its accounts. Foreign and local financial institutions, mutual funds and large domestic and multinational corporations would have never built a portfolio in Satyam Computers stocks if they were not satisfied with the competency and image of the company's statutory auditors. The PwC-Satyam combination offered the right choice to investors, discreet or speculative.

B Ramalinga Raju was not a scion of any Indian industry house of repute and tradition or business family such as Tatas, Birlas, Ambanis, Godrej, Bajaj, Munjal, Jindal, Arunachalam, Shivashailam, Goenkas, Mallyas and Mittals. Raju had a modest agricultural family background but was an extremely smart, highly ambitious and smooth talking first generation entrepreneur. He did not have the academic or technical brilliance of Infosys' N R Narayana Murthy or Tata Consultancy's Subramanian Ramadorai who helped build India's top two global IT corporations.

Few would have thought of investing in Raju's Satyam Computers if he did not produce attractive balance sheets year after year, or kept the right company in financial and political circles, locally and globally. He helped Hyderabad get the name of a tech-city. He was a business host to President Bill Clinton, who paid an official visit to Hyderabad, the first ever by a US president. The association of PwC provided Raju the right opportunity and strength to secure global focus for Satyam and for himself.

Like all its investors, Leena Mangat was never suspicious of the Satyam-Price Waterhouse joint run before she decided to invest a good part of her retirement benefits in Satyam stocks.

CHAPTER II

The Confession

It was an unprovoked and unsolicited confession that stunned the entire corporate world. The stock markets in India and the United States of America were shell-shocked. Close friends and colleagues of the Satyam Computers chairman told the media that Raju did not take anyone – not even his very near ones in the family – into confidence before making the confessional statement to the company's board of directors on 7 January 2009. There were others who believed he did it at the instance of Price Waterhouse.

PwC's India wing was nervous at the developments at Satyam after Raju's last ditch attempt to make Satyam Computers buy up two of the family-owned companies – Maytas Infrastructure and Maytas Properties – for a gross value of close to US$ 1.6 billion flopped due to severe resistance from Satyam's institutional shareholders. These institutional shareholders challenged an earlier Satyam board decision approving the executive management proposal to take over the two Maytas companies, ostensibly to clear the decks for diversification into infrastructure development and real estate business.

Ironically, the purchase value of the two Maytas companies matched the amount of financial fraud at Satyam. If the Maytas acquisition move had gone through, the financial fraud at Satyam would probably never have been unearthed. It is possible that Price Waterhouse may have helped Raju engineer the idea of taking the course of an 'in-house' acquisition to save their own backs along with Raju's. Interestingly, Maytas Properties engaged the services of another global audit and accounting major, Ernst & Young, for valuation of its assets. It was an intriguing move by Maytas, promoted by Raju's siblings. Read in the reverse order, Maytas is Satyam.

The following is the confession by Raju:

To the Board of Directors Satyam Computers Services Limited From B Ramalinga Raju Chairman, Satyam Computers Services Limited

7 January 2009

Dear Board Members,

It is with deep regret, and tremendous burden that I am carrying on my conscience, that I would like to bring the following facts to your notice:

1. **The balance sheet carries of September 30, 2008**
   a. **Inflated (non-existent) cash and bank balances of Rs 5,040 crores (as against Rs 5,361 crores reflected in the books).**
   b. **An accrued interest of Rs 376 crores which is non-existent.**
   c. **An understated liability of Rs 1,230 crores on account of funds arranged by me.**
   d. **An overstated debtors position of Rs 490 crores (as against Rs 2,651 reflected in the books).**
2. **For the September quarter (Q2) we reported a revenue of Rs 2,700 crores and an operating margin of Rs 649 crores (24 per cent of revenues) as against the actual revenues of Rs 2,112 crores and an actual operating margin of Rs 61 crores (3 per cent of revenues). This has resulted in artificial cash and bank balances going up by Rs 588 crores in Q2 alone.**

   The gap in the balance sheet has arisen purely on account of inflated profits over a period of last several years (limited only to

Satyam standalone, books of subsidiaries reflecting true performance). What started as a marginal gap between actual operating profit and the one reflected in the books of accounts continued to grow over the years. It has attained unmanageable proportions as the size of the company operations grew significantly (annualised revenue run rate of Rs 11,276 crores in the September quarter, 2008 and official reserves of Rs 8,392 crores).

The differential in the real profits and the one reflected in the books was further accentuated by the fact that the company had to carry additional resources and assets to justify higher level of operations – thereby significantly increasing the costs.

Every attempt made to eliminate the gap failed. As the promoters held a small percentage of equity, the concern was that poor performance would result in take-over, thereby exposing the gap. It was like riding a tiger, not knowing how to get off without being eaten.

The aborted Maytas acquisition deal was the last attempt to fill the fictitious assets with real ones. Maytas' investors were convinced that this is a good divestment opportunity and strategic fit. Once Satyam's problem was solved, it was hoped that Maytas' payments can be delayed. But that was not to be. What followed in the last several days is common knowledge.

I would like the Board to know:

1. That neither myself, nor the Managing Director (including our spouses) sold any shares in the last eight years – excepting for a small proportion declared and sold for philanthropic purposes.
2. That in the last two years a net amount of Rs 1,230 crore was arranged to Satyam (not reflected in the books of Satyam) to keep the operations going by resorting to pledging all the promoter shares and raising funds from known sources by giving all kinds of assurances (statement enclosed, only to the members of the board). Significant dividend payments, acquisitions, capital expenditure to provide for growth did not help matters. Every attempt was made to keep the wheel moving and to ensure prompt payment of salaries to the associates. The last straw was the selling

of most of the pledged shares by the lenders on account of margin triggers.

3. That neither me, nor the Managing Director took even one rupee/dollar from the company and have not benefited in financial terms on account of the inflated results.
4. None of the board members, past or present, had any knowledge of the situation in which the company is placed. Even business leaders and senior executives in the company, such as, Ram Mynampati, Subu D, T R Anand, Keshab Panda, Virender Agarwal, A S Murthy, Hari T, S V Krishnan, Vijay Prasad, Manish Mehta, Murli V, Sriram Papani, Kiran Kavale, Joe Lagioia, Ravindra Penumetsa, Jayaraman and Prabhakar Gupta are unaware of the real situation as against the books of accounts.

   None of my or Managing Director's immediate or extended family members has any idea about these issues. Having put these facts before you, I leave it to the wisdom of the board to take the matters forward.

However, I am also taking the liberty to recommend the following steps:

1. A task force has been formed in the last few days to address the situation arising out of the failed Maytas acquisition attempt. This consists of some of the most accomplished leaders of Satyam: Subu D, T R Anand, Keshab Panda and Virender Agarwal, representing business functions, and A S Murthy, Hari T and Murali V representing support functions. I suggest that Ram Mynampati be made the Chairman of this task force to immediately address some of the operational matters on hand. Ram can also act as an interim CEO reporting to the board.
2. Merrill Lynch can be entrusted with the task of quickly exploring some merger opportunities.
3. You may have a 'restatement of accounts' prepared by the auditors in light of the facts that I have placed before you. I have promoted and have been associated with Satyam for well over twenty years now. I have seen it grow from few people to 53,000 people, with 185 Fortune 500 companies as customers and operations in 66

countries. Satyam has established an excellent leadership and competency base at all levels. I sincerely apologise to all Satyamites and stakeholders, who have made Satyam a special organisation, for the current situation.

I am confident they will stand by the company in this hour of crisis. In the light of the above, I fervently appeal to the board to hold together to take some important steps. Mr T R Prasad is well placed to mobilise support from the government at this crucial time. With the hope that members of the task force and the financial advisor, Merrill Lynch (now Bank of America) will stand by the company at this crucial hour, I am marking copies of this statement to them as well.

Under the circumstances, I am tendering my resignation as the chairman of Satyam and shall continue in this position only till such time the current board is expanded. My continuance is just to ensure enhancement of the board over the next several days or as early as possible. I am now prepared to subject myself to the laws of the land and face consequences thereof.

(B Ramalinga Raju)

Notably, Raju made no mention of the company's independent auditors and audit partners leaving a clear doubt about their association and involvement in the case. The first part of Raju's confessional statement about the forged numbers in the company's balance sheet gives an impression that it was drafted by an expert financial accountant. The matter was brief and to the point. As the CBI investigation later exposed, the confession was only the tip of an ice-berg.

It was a master stroke by the Raju family, especially by Raju siblings Teja and Rama, who managed Maytas Infrastructure and Maytas Properties, to engage the services of Ernst & Young for valuation of Maytas Properties. Ironically, the job was performed very fast and in right earnest by Ernst & Young. The latter was associated with the audit function of Maytas Properties. In the minutes of the Satyam Computers board meeting on 16 December 2008, the company's chief financial officer (CFO) Srinivas Vadlamani, who was later arrested and sent to jail, had said that E&Y had valued the closely-held Maytas Properties for Rs 6,523 crores though Satyam Computers had agreed to acquire it for Rs 6,410 crores. The amount more than covered Ramalinga Raju's confessed 'inflated (non-existent) cash and bank balances of Rs 5,040 crores (as against Rs 5,361 crores reflected in the books)' at the end of September 2008 and provided a cushion to cover additional liability until 31 December 2008.

Did E&Y inflate the valuation of Maytas Properties to suit Raju's game plan? Did the global financial audit and consultancy firm play ball with Ramalinga Raju, a former recipient of E&Y's annual 'Entrepreneur of the Year' award? These are tricky questions for which there may never be satisfactory answers. The closely-held Maytas Properties' last reported annual turnover was only around Rs 22 crores.

Unlike Price Waterhouse and its US principals who refused to own responsibility for book-cooking at Satyam Computers and practically disassociated themselves with the management of their Indian audit operations with regard to the role of the firm's partners in the Satyam accountancy fraud, E&Y stood by its valuation of the assets of Satyam properties. However, the government of India in its submission before the Company Law Board (CLB) pooh-poohed the E&Y claim. "How hollow this valuation is…As per our knowledge, the company (Maytas Properties) does not have any land bank and this company, having a turnover of mere Rs 22 crores, was valued at Rs 6,523 crores," an official appearing for the government told CLB during a hearing on the Maytas Properties case. The matter was reported by the news agency, Press Trust of India (PTI), from New Delhi on 25 February 2009.

The government alleged that E&Y took just a day to do the valuation of Maytas properties. CLB chairman S Balasubramanian asked the government representative if the "entire valuation was done in a week". To this, the government official's reply was: "the valuation was done in a day only." The government alleged fraud in the valuation. It said that E&Y had valued all the 31 projects of Maytas in Chennai, Hyderabad, Bangalore and Nagpur. "In fact, Maytas Properties does not have any land. Some of its subsidiary companies have development rights, not lands." The government representative further alleged that in violation of the established accounting norms, Satyam appointed an advocate, Raghavendra Rao, to help E&Y during valuation. "Rao was given Rs 40 lakhs by the company and Ernst & Young got only Rs 10 lakhs for the entire exercise," a government representative added.

E&Y denied all the allegations. It said the firm had "taken considerably more time, which we believe was adequate and also have significant evidence to the effect". Earlier an E&Y spokesperson made a counter allegation in the media that Satyam Computers improperly used the valuation for its merger with the IT company. She said the firm was told that the valuation of Maytas Properties was for a proposed share transaction involving the existing shareholders of the company. "We were not given to understand by any party, explicitly or implicitly, during the valuation exercise about Satyam's plan to acquire Maytas Properties."

E&Y also said that it was engaged by a law firm and not by Satyam for the valuation which is mandatory for such share transaction, according to the guidelines laid down by the Reserve Bank of India (RBI). "This valuation was done only to comply with RBI's regulatory requirements and our engagement letter and valuation report clearly and unequivocally stated this." E&Y also clarified that though it was associated with the audit of Maytas Properties, the firm was not the auditor of various subsidiaries the company floated to acquire real estate assets. "Since Maytas Properties is not listed (with stock exchange), there was no requirement to prepare a consolidated statement and audit it." In another public statement, E&Y said "we would like to again clarify that we were not engaged by Satyam Computers Services Limited or any of its subsidiaries to conduct the valuation of Maytas Properties and learnt of the Maytas/Satyam transaction after it was announced publicly".

However, there were not many takers of E&Y's explanations, not the government for certain..The valuation amount, Rs 6,523 crores (US$ 1.4 billion), was too close to the sum Raju needed to get himself bailed out of the financial fraud he committed in Satyam. Moreover, Raju's land bank was regarded by many as a myth. The opinion was divided about the amount of land under the actual (not virtual) legal possession of Maytas Properties. The government itself had challenged the Maytas claim. The development right of land has little meaning without its legal ownership.

Ironically, both Satyam and Maytas Properties chose to maintain silence on E&Y's public statements and clarifications. Some felt that the Maytas valuation was part of a huge conspiracy involving the Satyam chairman, his CFO and the two global audit and financial consultancy majors, PwC and E&Y, to cover up the US$ 1.6 billion fraud in the Hyderabad-headquartered IT company. If the financial conspiracy between Satyam and Maytas went unchallenged, Raju would have a great tiger ride before he got off without being eaten or harmed.

Ramalinga Raju's confession prompted a series of investigations by both the government and its Serious Frauds Office and other independent agencies such as SEBI, ICAI and New York Stock Exchange. We "need to check whether the audit was done properly", said SEBI chairman C B Bhave. PwC's instant reaction was it was examining Raju's statement but could not comment further due to confidentiality issues. The bookkeeping fraud could cause serious problem for PwC in the US, where Satyam is listed, Investors there were certainly expected to turn to the courts for recompense and there are legal precedents for holding auditors accountable.

Ramalinga Raju's confession raised certain basic questions on the reliability of the company's accounts, the roles played (or not played) by both internal and external auditors, banks, credit rating agencies, the office of the regional provident fund commissioner responsible for collection of the provident fund (PF) contribution by employees as well as the employer (Satyam), income-tax department, SEBI and the Department of Corporate Affairs of the government of India. It also rubbished the company's proudly pronounced accounting policy, tall claims in the directors' report and the auditor's report and pompous statement by the Satyam Computers chairman.

It also showed the hollowness of 'Corporate Awards' given by various institutions and organisations for 'leadership' and 'governance' without independent verification of a company's so-called achievements. Ramalinga Raju and his Satyam received one after another coveted corporate awards from some of the country's top business rating organisations. The company received the 'Golden Peacock Global Award' for Excellence in Corporate Governance in 2008, a month after the World Bank banned all contracts to Satyam for a period of eight years over charges of corruption by way of providing improper benefits to bank staff and for failing to maintain documentation to support fees charged for its subcontractors The award is instituted by the World Council for Corporate Governance. The former Swedish Prime Minister, Dr Ola Ullsten, was the lead judge.

The Satyam management is also alleged to have used its money power to influence political leaders across party lines, the income-tax department, the government of the State of Andhra Pradesh and the Union Government. In February 2009, an investigating officer looking into tax irregularities of Satyam Computers complained of interference by influential political groups to thwart her investigation. A Satyam-promoted health charity, Emergency Management & Research Institute, was faced with corruption charges for misuse of government funds it received under the National Health Mission and land grab.

An accounting fraud of this magnitude did not take place in a single year. It accumulated itself over a period of time through systematic misrepresentation of financial statements. One of the most interesting parts of these statements is the fudging of the company's employment register, which carried the names of some 5,000-6,000 'ghost' employees or non-existent employees. These 'ghost' employees may have contributed significantly to the company's inflated income as well as expenditure. The special audit by CBI had implied the impact of the inflated income statement on the balance sheet. The company's auditors, Price Waterhouse, routinely complimented the Satyam management for maintaining "an adequate internal control system commensurate with the size of the company". The audit firm was either blind or too complacent with the internal control system to take note of the irregularities and did not consider the need for any cross-check.

The company's annual reports were full of lies carefully wrapped under 'feel good' statements, auditor's and directors' reports that fooled Satyam's stakeholders, the concerned government agencies and the regulatory authorities year after year. They were crafted by top brains in the business and were taken on their face value by all. Samples of the company's accounting policy, auditor's report, chairman's speech, directors' report and notes to accounts, all from the company's last annual report for the accounting year ended 31 March 2008, under Ramalinga Raju are provided in the pages that follow.

EXCERPTS FROM SATYAM'S 2008 ANNUAL ACCOUNTS

Accounting Policy Year: March 2008

a) Basis of Presentation

The financial statements of the Company are prepared under historical cost convention in accordance with the Generally Accepted Accounting Principles (GAAP) applicable in India and the provisions of the Indian Companies Act, 1956.

b) Use of Estimates

The preparation of the financial statements in conformity with the GAAP requires that the management makes estimates and assumptions that affect the reported amounts of assets and liabilities, disclosure of contingent liabilities as at the date of the financial statements, and the reported amounts of revenue and expenses during the reported period/year. Actual results could differ from those estimates.

c) Revenue Recognition

Revenue from professional services consists primarily of revenue earned from services performed on a time and material basis.

The related revenue is recognised as and when the services are performed. The Company also performs time bound fixed-price engagements, under which revenue is recognised using the percentage of completion method of accounting.

The cumulative impact of any revision in estimates of the percentage of work completed is reflected in the year in which the change becomes known. Provisions for estimated losses on such engagements are made during the period/year in which a loss becomes probable and can be reasonably estimated.

Amounts received or billed in advance of services performed are recorded as advance from customers/unearned revenue. Unbilled revenue, included in debtors, represents amounts recognised based on services performed in advance of billing in accordance with contract terms.

d) Fixed Assets

Fixed assets are stated at actual cost less accumulated depreciation. The actual cost capitalised includes material cost, freight, installation cost, duties and taxes, finance charges and other incidental expenses incurred during the construction/installation stage.

Depreciation on fixed assets is computed on the straight line method over their estimated useful lives at the rates which are higher than the rates prescribed under Schedule XIV of the Companies Act, 1956. Individual assets acquired for less than Rs 5,000 are entirely depreciated in the period/year of acquisition.

The cost of and the accumulated depreciation of fixed assets sold, retired or otherwise disposed off are removed from the stated values and the resulting gains and losses are included in the profit and loss account.

Costs of application software for internal use are generally charged to revenue as incurred due to its estimated useful lives being relatively short, usually less than one year.

Capital work in progress

Assets under installation or under construction as at the Balance Sheet date are shown as Capital Work in progress. Advances paid towards acquisition of assets are also included under Capital Work in progress.

e) Investments

Investments are classified into current investments and long-term investments. Current investments are carried at the lower of cost and market value. Any reduction in carrying amount and any reversals of such reductions are charged or credited to the profit and loss account.

Long-term investments are carried at cost less provision made to recognise any decline, other than temporary, in the value of such investments.

f) Foreign Currency Translation

Transactions in foreign currency are recorded at exchange rate prevailing on the date of transaction. Monetary assets and liabilities denominated in foreign currency are translated at the rate of exchange at the balance sheet date and resultant gain or loss is recognised in the profit and loss account.

Non-monetary assets and liabilities are translated at the rate prevailing on the date of transaction.

The operations of foreign branches of the company are of integral in nature and the financial statements of these branches are translated using the same principles and procedures as those of head office.

Gain or loss on forward exchange contract is computed by multiplying the foreign currency amount of the forward exchange contract by the difference between the forward rate available at the reporting date for the remaining maturity of the contract and the contracted forward rate (or the forward rate last used to measure a gain or loss on that contract for an earlier period), is recognised in the profit and loss account of the period/year.

Gain/Loss on settlement of transaction arising on cancellation or renewal of a forward exchange contract is recognised as income or as expense of the period/year.

Pursuant to ICAI Announcement Accounting for Derivatives on the early adoption of Accounting Standard AS 30 Financial Instruments: Recognisation and Measurement, the Company has early adopted the standard for the year under review, to the extent that the adoption does not conflict with existing mandatory accounting standards and other authoritative pronouncements, Company Law and other regulatory requirements.

g) Employee Benefits

Contributions to defined Schemes such as Provident Fund, Employee State Insurance Scheme and Superannuation are charged as incurred on accrual basis. The Company also provides for gratuity and leave encashment in accordance with the requirements of revised Accounting Standard – 15 Employee Benefits based on actuarial valuation carried out as at the balance sheet date.

h) Taxes on Income

Tax expense for the year comprises of current tax and deferred tax. Current taxes are measured at the amounts expected to be paid using the applicable tax rates and tax laws. Deferred tax assets and liabilities are measured using tax rates and tax laws that have been enacted or substantively enacted by the balance sheet date. The effect on deferred tax assets and liabilities of a change in tax rates is recognised in the profit and loss account in the period/year of change. Deferred tax assets and deferred tax liabilities are recognised for the future tax consequences attributable to differences between the financial statements carrying amounts of existing assets and liabilities and their respective tax bases and operating loss carry forwards.

i) Earnings per Share

The earnings considered in ascertaining the Company's Earnings Per Share (EPS) comprises the net profit after tax (and includes the post tax effect of any extra ordinary items).

Basic EPS is the weighted average number of shares outstanding during the period/year. The number of shares used in computing Diluted EPS comprises of weighted average shares considered for deriving Basic EPS, and also the weighted average number of equity shares which could have been issued on the conversion of all dilutive potential equity shares. Dilutive potential equity shares are deemed converted as of the beginning of the period/year, unless they have been issued at a later date. The diluted potential equity shares have been adjusted for the proceeds receivable had the shares been actually issued at fair value (i.e. average market value of the outstanding shares). The number of shares and potentially dilutive shares are adjusted for share splits/reverse share splits and bonus shares, as appropriate.

j) Associate Stock Option Scheme

Stock options granted to the associates under the stock option schemes established after 19 June, 1999 are evaluated as per the accounting treatment prescribed by Employee Stock Option Scheme and Employee Stock Purchase Scheme Guidelines, 1999 issued by Securities and Exchange Board of India. Accordingly, the excess of market value of the stock options as on the date of grant over the exercise price of the options is recognised as deferred employee compensation and is charged to profit and loss account on graded vesting basis over the vesting period of the options. The employee stock option outstanding is shown under Reserves and Surplus.

k) Research and Development

Revenue expenditure incurred on research and development is charged to revenue in the year/period in which it is incurred. Assets used for research and development activities are included in fixed assets.

Auditors' Report

Auditor's Report Year End: March 2008

1. We have audited the attached Balance Sheet of Satyam Computers Services Limited (the Company), as at 31 March, 2008, and the related Profit and Loss Account and Cash Flow Statement for the year ended on that date annexed thereto, which we have signed under reference to this report. These financial statements are the responsibility of the Company's management. Our responsibility is to express an opinion of these financial statements based on our audit.

2. We conducted our audit in accordance with the auditing standards generally accepted in India. Those Standards require that we plan and perform the audit to obtain reasonable assurance about whether the financial statements are free of material misstatement. An audit includes examining, on a test basis, evidence supporting the amounts and disclosures in the financial statements. An audit also includes assessing the accounting principles used and significant estimates made by management, as well as evaluating the overall financial statement presentation. We believe that our audit provides a reasonable basis for our opinion.

3. As required by the Companies (Auditors Report) Order, 2003, as amended by the Companies (Auditors Report) (Amendment)

Order, 2004, issued by the Central Government of India in terms of sub-section (4A) of Section 227 of The Companies Act, 1956 of India (the Act) and on the basis of such checks of the books and records of the Company as we considered appropriate and according to the information and explanations given to us, we give in the Annexure a statement on the matters specified in paragraphs 4 and 5 of the said Order.

4. Further to our comments in the Annexure referred to in paragraph 3 above, we report that:
   (a) We have obtained all the information and explanations, which to the best of our knowledge and belief were necessary for the purposes of our audit;

   (b) In our opinion, proper books of account as required by law have been kept by the Company so far as appears from our examination of those books;

   (c) The Balance Sheet, Profit and Loss Account and Cash Flow Statement dealt with by this report are in agreement with the books of account;

   (d) In our opinion, the Balance Sheet, Profit and Loss Account and Cash Flow Statement dealt with by this report comply with the accounting standards referred to in sub-section (3C) of section 211 of the Act;

   (e) On the basis of written representations received from the directors, as on 31 March, 2008 and taken on record by the Board of Directors, none of the directors is disqualified as on 31 March, 2008 from being appointed as a director in terms of clause (g) of sub-section (1) of section 274 of the Act;

(f) In our opinion and to the best of our information and according to the explanations given to us, the said financial statements together with the notes thereon and attached thereto give in the prescribed manner the information required by the Act and give a true and fair view in conformity with the accounting principles generally accepted in India:

(i) in the case of the Balance Sheet, of the state of affairs of the Company as at 31 March, 2008;

(ii) in the case of the Profit and Loss Account, of the profit for the year ended on that date; and

(iii) in the case of the Cash Flow Statement, of the cash flows for the year ended on that date.

Annexure to the Auditors Report

[Referred to in paragraph 3 of the Auditors Report of even date to the members of Satyam Computers Services Limited on the financial statements as at and for the year ended March 31, 2008]

1. (a) The company is maintaining proper records showing full particulars including quantitative details and situation of fixed assets.

(b) The fixed assets are physically verified by the management according to a phased programme designed to cover all the items over a period of three years, which in our opinion, is reasonable having regard to the size of the company and the nature of its assets. Pursuant to the programme, a portion of the fixed assets has been physically verified by the management during the year and no material discrepancies between the book records and the physical inventory have been noticed.

(c) In our opinion and according to the information and explanations given to us, a substantial part of fixed assets has not been disposed of by the company during the year.

2. The company has not granted/taken any loans, secured or unsecured, to/from companies, firms or other parties covered in the register maintained under Section 301 of the Act.
3. In our opinion and according to the information and explanations given to us, having regard to the explanation that certain items purchased are of special nature for which suitable alternative sources do not exist for obtaining comparative quotations, there is an adequate internal control system commensurate with the size of the company and the nature of its business for the purchase of fixed assets and for the sale of services. The activities of the company do not involve Purchase of inventory and sale of goods. Further, on the basis of our examination of the books and records of the company, and according to the information and explanations given to us, we have neither come across nor have been informed of any continuing failure to correct major weaknesses in the aforesaid internal control system.
4. According to the information and explanations given to us, there have been no contracts or arrangements referred to in Section 301 of the Act during the year to be entered in the register required to be maintained under that section. Accordingly, commenting on transactions made in pursuance of such contracts or arrangements does not arise.
5. The company has not accepted any deposits from the public within the meaning of Sections 58A and 58AA of the Act and the rules framed there under.
6. In our opinion, the company has an internal audit system commensurate with its size and nature of its business.
7. (a) According to the information and explanations given to us and the records of the company examined by us, in our

opinion, the company is generally regular in depositing the undisputed statutory dues including provident fund, investor education and protection fund, employees state insurance, income-tax, sales-tax, wealth tax, service tax, customs duty and other material statutory dues as applicable with the appropriate authorities. According to the information and explanations given to us and the records of the company examined by us, excise duty and cess are not applicable to the company for the current year.

(b) According to the information and explanations given to us and the records of the company examined by us, the particulars of dues of Income Tax as at 31 March, 2008 which have not been deposited on account of dispute, are as follows:

According to the information and explanations given to us and the records of the company examined by us, there are no dues of Sales Tax, wealth tax, service tax, customs duty which have not been deposited on account of any dispute. According to the information and explanations given to us and the records of the company examined by us, excise duty and cess are not applicable to the company for the current year.

Name of the statute	Nature of dues	Amount (Rs)
Income Tax Act, 1961	Tax and Interest on disallowance of loss in one of the STPs and disallowance of excess claim U/s Section 10A.	13,35,05,579

Period to which the amount relates	Forum where the dispute is pending
2002-03	The Commissioner of Income Tax (Appeals)-I, Hyderabad

8. The company has no accumulated losses as at 31 March, 2008 and it has not incurred any cash losses in the financial year ended on that date or in the immediately preceding financial year.
9. According to the records of the company examined by us and the information and explanation given to us, the company has not defaulted in repayment of dues to any financial institution or bank or debenture holders as at the balance sheet date.
10. The company has not granted any loans and advances on the basis of security by way of pledge of shares, debentures and other securities.
11. In our opinion, the company is not a dealer or trader in shares, securities, debentures and other investments.
12. In our opinion and according to the information and explanations given to us, the terms and conditions of the guarantees given by the company, for loans taken by others from banks or financial institutions during the year, are not prejudicial to the interest of the company.
13. The company has not obtained any term loans.
14. On the basis of an overall examination of the balance sheet of the company, in our opinion and according to the information and explanations given to us, there are no funds raised on a short-term basis which have been used for long-term investment.
15. The company has not made any preferential allotment of shares to parties and companies covered in the register maintained under Section 301 of the Act during the year.
16. The company has not raised any money by public issues during the year.
17. During the course of our examination of the books and records of the company, carried out in accordance with the generally accepted auditing practices in India, and according to the information and explanations given to us, we have neither come across any instance of fraud on or by the company, noticed or

reported during the year, nor have we been informed of such case by the management.

18. The other clauses (ii), (iii) (b), (iii) (c), (iii) (d), (iii) (f), (iii) (g), (viii), (xiii), and (xix) of paragraph 4 of the Companies (Auditors Report) Order 2003, as amended by the Companies (Auditors Report) (Amendment) Order, 2004 are not applicable in the case of the company for the current year, since in our opinion there is no matter which arises to be reported in the aforesaid order.

Srinivas Talluri, Partner
Membership No. 29864
for and on behalf of
Price Waterhouse
Chartered Accountants

Place: Hyderabad
Date: 21 April 2008

Chairman's Speech Year: March 2008

Fiscal 2008 was an outstanding year for Satyam. We achieved record revenues and record net income. We expanded into new geographies and launched many more new, higher-value services. We acquired high-end firms that significantly strengthened our consulting capabilities, and we extended our lead in enterprise systems. We employed a record number of associates while bringing attrition to a three year low, and we were recognised as the best company in the world for associate training and development. We repositioned our brand and launched a strategic new global marketing sponsorship. We are now serving more clients – especially among the Fortune 500 – in more industries and more countries than ever in our history, and we are achieving uncommon success with our social responsibility programs.

I can think of no better way to mark the twentieth anniversary of Satyams founding than to report these results to you.

US GAAP revenues grew 46 percent, to US$ 14 billion, up from US$ 1.46 billion in fiscal 2007. While it took us 18 years to reach the US billion mark, we crossed the US billion threshold less than two years later. Our net income also grew by 40 percent last fiscal year, to US$ 7 million.

This growth has been the result of several strategic initiatives and continuous investments in our business model. It is also encouraging to note that last years exceptional results occurred despite a fairly hostile macroeconomic environment: the rupee appreciated by almost 9 percent and our main cost component-talent-continued to rise. To curtail these margin pressures, we focused on increasing billing rates and offshore revenue contributions, diversifying our regional revenue mix. These initiatives worked: North America contributed 60.35 percent of our revenue in fiscal 2008, down from 64.53 percent in the previous year.

Our goal has always been to delight all of our stakeholders-investors, customers, associates and society at large. Our strategies are clearly aligned in this direction and have achieved superior results.

Among Satyams most important and prominent developments in fiscal 2008 was the repositioning of Satyams brand to address market demands and to reflect the higher-value capabilities we developed or acquired over the past several years.

Our clients now expect us to work with them to transform their key business processes, their skill sets and cultures, their organisations and business models – as well as their technology – to help them achieve significant improvements in their performance. To communicate that mission, focus and experience, Satyam updated its corporate tagline to Business Transformation Together.

To help promote that positioning worldwide – even more in Europe, Asia Pacific and Latin America – we entered into a strategic partnership with FIFA, footballs governing organisation.

Satyam is now the official IT Services Provider to the 2010 and 2014 World Cups, to be held in South Africa and Brazil, respectively. The World Cup is the largest and most-viewed sporting event in the world. In conjunction with the partnership, we have also launched a global sports management practice.

During the year, we continued to expand our service delivery footprint, opening new centres in Australia, Malaysia, China, Egypt and Brazil, and we launched new, advanced industry-and domain-specific solutions in areas such as BPO, engineering services, infrastructure management, analytics and consulting. Ten times during the year, industry analysts have ranked Satyam's offerings among the best in our industry.

Our customers have embraced these developments, and our efforts to strengthen our customer relationships have gained significant traction. Satyam now has two customers with an annual revenue run rate greater than USD million, and more than 50 exceeding USD million. While we continue to strengthen our existing relationships, efforts to cultivate new customers have also gained momentum. At the end of fiscal 2008, Satyam had 617 active clients, with more than 180 on the US and Global Fortune 500.

Our ability to acquire and retain talented professionals has also been exemplary. Today, Satyam has more than 51,000 employees, and our annualised attrition rate in Q4 was 11.5 percent-among the industry's lowest. Our excellent retention is a result of our considerable efforts to provide excellent career and leadership opportunities, efforts recognised by the American Society for Training and Development last year when they named Satyam the single best company in the world for associate development – the first time a non-American company was ever cited for this honour.

Superior innovation is also fundamental to Satyams success, and draws on our culture of continuous learning. The capacity to innovate is a primary determinant of market value for companies like ours.

A new venture with Cisco Systems, Inc. is an example of innovation that resulted in a transformational opportunity. The venture provides secure medical and emergency management services to local and national governments, among other segments. The services are built on advanced – yet proven – processes and technology, and are designed to be replicated and implemented across the world.

Innovation extends to how we build our capabilities. From this perspective, we made four key acquisitions in fiscal 2008. In 02, we acquired Nitor Global Solutions, a UK-based infrastructure management services firm to bolster our growing remote IMS capabilities. Nitor helps customers design, implement and manage Microsoft technologies. In 03, we acquired Bridge Strategy Group, a high-end, US-based management consulting firm. Bridge strengthens our business strategy formulation and business transformation capabilities and provides us expanded access to additional clients, at higher levels.

In the fourth quarter, we entered into a definitive agreement with S&V Management Consultants, a renowned, Belgium-based supply chain management consulting firm that ARC Advisory Group ranks among the world's premier boutique SCM consulting companies. And, to augment our capabilities in the increasingly important market research and customer analytics field, we acquired Caterpillars Market Research and Customer Analytics Business, including its intellectual property.

I am pleased to report that MZ Consult, a global investor relations and financial communications firm, included Satyam among the five organisations it determined to have the Best IR Website in the Asia Pacific and Africa regions. Satyam also earned the top ranking in the global technology industry for Best Earnings Release and Financial Disclosures Procedures. Additionally, we were named among the region's top two companies for Best Corporate Governance Practices.

Additionally, in January, we listed our existing ADSs on the NYSE Euronext stock exchange in Amsterdam. The listing has made investing in Satyam easier, enabled extended trading, and enhanced the organisations visibility in Europe.

I am confident that as we continue to work more closely with clients on their most strategic and critical transformation initiatives, we will both succeed, and Satyam's excellent growth will continue. Against this backdrop, we look forward to a revenue growth rate of 24 to 26 percent in fiscal 2009 (in both Indian and US GAAP). While EPS is expected to grow between 17 and 19 percent in Indian GAAP EPADS is expected to grow from 15.2 to 17.6 percent, as per US GAAP. The Board has proposed a final dividend of 125 percent. The total dividend for fiscal year 2008 stands at 175 percent.

> The extraordinary successes I described here are the results of some 51,000 associates who embody Satyam's values of entrepreneurship collaboration, inventiveness and responsibility. I am proud to count myself among them, and I look forward to working with them, with our clients, and with you as we take Satyam into its next twenty years

Best regards,

B Ramalinga Raju

Place: Hyderabad
Date: 21 April 2008

Directors' Report

Directors Report Year End: March 2008

The directors are pleased to present their report for the financial year 2007-08.

Financial highlights Rs in crores

Particulars	2007-08	2006-07	Growth%
Income from software services	8,137.28	6,228.47	30.65
Other income	257.20	181.61	41.62
Total income	8,394.48	6,410.08	30.96
Operating profit (PBIDT)	2,085.74	1,710.73	21.92
Interest	5.94	7.61	(21.94)
Depreciation	137.94	129.89	6.20
Profit before tax	1,941.86	1,573.23	23.43
Provision for tax	226.12	150.00	50.75
Profit after tax	1,715.74	1,423.23	20.55
Equity share capital	134.10	133.44	0.49
Reserves	7,221.71	5,648.07	27.86
Transfer to general reserve	171.60	142.32	20.57
Earnings per share (Rs Per equity share of Rs 2 each)			
— Basic (Rs)	25.66	21.73	18.08
— Diluted EPS (Rs)	25.12	21.25	18.21
Dividend rate (Interim plus Final) (%)	175		175

Overview

For the financial year ended 31 March, 2008, your Company reported a total income of Rs 8,394.48 crores, comprising income from software services of Rs 8,137.28 crores, and other income of Rs 257.20 crores. Total revenues grew by 30.65% over the previous financial year. The company recorded an operating profit of Rs 2,085.74 crores, and a net profit of Rs 1,715.74 crores, representing a growth of 21.92% and 20.55% respectively, over the previous financial year. North America, Europe and rest of the world accounted for 60.35%, 20.58% and 19.07% of the revenues, respectively. Offshore revenue during the year was 51.84%, while onsite was 48.16%.

Dividend

Your directors recommended a final dividend of Rs 2.50 per share for your approval. This, coupled with the interim dividend of Re 1 per share already paid, raises the total dividend for the year to Rs 3.50 per share.

Increase in the share capital

During the year under review, the paid-up share capital of the Company increased from Rs 133.44 crores divided into 667,196,009 equity shares of Rs 2 each to Rs 134.10 crores divided into 670,479,293 equity shares of Rs 2 each, consequent to issue of 3,283,284 equity shares of Rs 2 each to Associates upon exercise of options under the stock option plans of the Company.

Listing on Euronext

In a path-setting initiative, your Company listed its existing ADSs with Euronext Stock Exchange (NYSEs European trading platform). With this move, Satyam became the first Indian company to list on three major trading platforms around the world, making it a truly globally-tradeable entity. The listing was also the first of its kind globally, under the fast-track mechanism. Europe is a dynamic and growing market for your Company and our listing will demonstrate our continued and growing commitment to the region.

Human resources

The total number of Associates on 31 March, 2008 was 45,969, against 35,670 on 31 March, 2007. The attrition rate for the year 2007-08 was 13.09%.

Your Company believes that today a major HR challenge for any organisation is capability building and enhancement and associate engagement. Your Company continued to work toward these three components through various initiatives, such as:

Building capability through collaboration with institutions at the national and international levels, and via campus link programs.

Capability enhancement by realigning leadership competency frameworks to new business realities and the company's future roadmap.

Delighting associates through empowerment, unique organisation design and enablement of social participation for better productivity and less attrition.

Satyam Learning World: The emergence of knowledge economies has made learning and leadership critical. Satyam Learning World is the enterprise-wide learning ecosystem that captures and delivers the learning and development needs of the entire corporation through a single platform. Satyam Learning Centre and Satyam School of Leadership, the two pillars of this ecosystem, are the learning and development partners of businesses across Satyam, each having a well-defined mandate.

More than 70% of all learning at Satyam is delivered virtually. We have a carefully designed learning and development strategy to meet the entire life cycle of learning and development of our Associates, from entry-level personnel to senior leaders. The SSLs vision is to make Satyam one of the top five organisations in the world in building global Associates, through effective learning and development.

Further, our globally distributed workforce warrants the application of pervasive and potent communication technologies to ensure accessibility of learning and development initiatives to all associates. Through the newly launched Web Radio/TV station called Planet Satyam, more than 50,000 associates across the globe have access to an entire range of learning and development programs via a mouse click. A first-of-its-kind initiative in the industry, Planet Satyam takes the organisation's learning programs to another level of accessibility, convenience and inclusiveness. Complimenting the traditional model of classroom-based learning and development programmes, it significantly virtualises the learning ecosystem.

Infrastructure

During the year under review, your Company continued to create best-in-class infrastructure facilities to support its growth strategies and has added 10,000 spaces, an increase of approximately 25% over the previous year. Of these, more than 40% have been created in own campuses at different locations. The Company has established base for the first time in a Tier 2 city, i.e. Vishakha-patham in Andhra Pradesh. We have also established new development centres in Egypt, Malaysia and Nanjing in China and new marketing offices in Singapore and Sydney.

During the current year, we will develop infrastructure in the SEZ campuses at two locations in Hyderabad and one location each in Chennai and Nagpur, in addition to taking on leased SEZ spaces in Hyderabad, Bangalore, Chennai and Pune.

Network and Systems: Your Company continuously focuses on upgrading SatyamNet, its sophisticated high-speed data, voice and other communicating network, to keep pace with contemporary global trends. Your directors are happy to state that during the year under review, the Company has successfully undertaken technological upgrade in the wide areas of networking, security, business continuity and collaboration tools.

Quality

Quality is an integral part of everything that we do at Satyam. It implies the right Processes, Service Offerings and Projects are operating at the highest levels of maturity and are benchmarked with best niche players.

Your company has set benchmarks by developing and deploying simple, efficient and effective processes related to Health Safety & Environment (HSE) in accordance with ISO 14001 and OHSAS 18001 standards. Your company has received Payment Card Industry (PCI DSS 1.1) certification for its banking sub-vertical operations. And, as part of ongoing efforts to reinforce the quality culture and customer orientation, your company has successfully implemented Quality Management Systems (QMS) certification for all associates.

Your company has a comprehensive Business Continuity and Disaster Recovery framework in place to prevent and contain potential business disruptions in the event of disaster. It can quickly resume services to customers acceptable service levels. Your company has also established leadership through participation and sharing of best practices in industry forums on Business Continuity Management.

Six Sigma has been the main driver of continuous improvements and customer delight this year, with 2,200 Six Sigma projects implemented for new process definitions and solutions to business problems. A total of 2,200 associates are certified as Green Beits, Black Belts and Master Black Belts.

Moving forward, your company will continue to endeavour to implement and institutionalise best-in-class systems and processes to achieve delivery excellence and stakeholder delight.

Awards and recognitions

Some of the recognitions your Company earned during 2007-08 are listed below.

Satyam has been ranked No. 1 in the American Society for Training and Development (ASTD's) annual BEST awards programme for 2007. This made Satyam the first non-US organisation and the first in Asia to earn the top ranking. Satyam was top among 103 organisations from in eight countries. The BEST awards recognise organisations that demonstrate enterprise-wide success through employee learning and development.

Satyam has earned a Most Admired Knowledge Enterprise (MAKE) award – as a top Asian Knowledge Organisation – for the second year in a row. The MAKE awards are given to leading Asian organisations that leverage enterprise knowledge to create value through innovation, product or service excellence, and operational effectiveness.

Satyam also won the Partner of the Year 2007 Award for Acquired Applications from Oracle. The award recognises Satyam's capabilities in building new competencies quickly and its ability to add value to Oracle, its customers, and products.

Satyam won the VIP (Vision, Impact, and Progress) Award in the IMPACT category from Computer Associates Business Service Optimisation (BSO). The Impact Award recognises demonstrable and measurable results from improved IT, especially in terms of productivity, financial benefits quality improvements and/or customer satisfaction.

Satyam became the first Indian Service Integrator to win the prestigious Competitive Strategy Leadership Award for Offshore Testing Market from Frost & Sullivan, a leading International research and consulting company. The organisation honoured Satyam in the Thought Leadership Quadrant in the testing space.

A Brown-Wilson survey ranked Satyam No. 1 among Indian IT services providers and No. 3 globally (based on cumulative rankings for years 2004 through 2007). Satyam was selected from among 1,455 outsourcing vendors in 77 countries in a survey published in *The Black Book of Outsourcing*. Satyam also ranked No. 1 globally on the following sub categories: ITO: Application Services; ITO: Process Consulting; ITO: Business Intelligence & Data Warehousing; ITO: Full Service ERP: SAP/Oracle/

PeopleSoft/JD Edwards; ESO: Integrated Solutions; ESO: Full-Service PLM /End-to-End.

Satyam was Citizenship Partner of the Year at the Microsoft Worldwide Partner Conference Awards. The Citizenship Partner of the Year recognises exceptional partners that have made a sustained commitment to society and their communities and can demonstrate the impact of their work.

Chairman B Ramalinga Raju won the Ernst & Young Entrepreneur of the Year Award. Raju was selected for this honour for his business acumen and efforts to enhance the community.

Corporate Governance

Your Company retained its eminent position in the 2008 Investor Relations Global Rankings for the Asia, Pacific and Africa Region and won the following recognitions:

- IR Website: Top 5 in region
- Corporate Governance Practices: Top 2 in region
- Financial Disclosure Procedures: Top 5 in region; First in Technology; and First in India

A report on Corporate Governance, along with Auditors certificate in compliance with clause 49 of the listing agreement, is provided elsewhere in the Annual Report.

Subsidiaries

Ministry of Company Affairs vide their letter dated 29 February, 2008 granted approval under section 212 (8) of the Companies Act, 1956 exempting the Company from attaching the documents of subsidiaries as specified under section 212 (1) of the Companies Act, 1956. Accordingly, the documents as referred above are not attached to the Balance Sheet. However, the summarised financial information of the subsidiaries is published elsewhere in this Annual Report-2007-08, for information of members of the Company.

The name of Nipuna Services Ltd., subsidiary of the Company, has been changed to Satyam BPO Ltd. effective 28 December, 2007. During the year under review, your Company acquired equity shares of Satyam BPO held by the strategic investors and consequently, it has become wholly owned subsidiary effective 31 December, 2007.

During the year under review, your Company has set up subsidiaries viz., Satyam Computers Services Egypt in Cairo, Egypt and SATYAM SERVICOS DE INFORMATICA LTDA in Brazil, to tap further potential business opportunities. Further, your Company incorporated its second subsidiary in Nanjing, China viz. Satyam Computers Services (Nanjing) Company Ltd.

In line with the organisations strategy to add higher value service offerings, bridge competency gaps, enhance leadership capabilities, add sound and significant customer relationships and to strengthen the brand, your Company has been making acquisitions in various industry verticals and technology spaces. During the year under review, your Company acquired Nitor Global Solutions Limited (Nitor), UK, a niche consulting firm providing Infrastructure Management. Services (IMS) and Bridge Strategy Group (BSG), an US-based management consulting firm.

Consequently, Nitor and BSG became subsidiaries effective 4 January, 2008 and 4 April, 2008, respectively.

On 21 April, 2008, your Board of directors approved the acquisition of:

i) S&V Management Consultants (S&V) a Belgium-based SCM strategy consulting firm in Supply Chain Management area for a total consideration of Rs 141.5 crores (equivalent US$ 35.5 million). The acquisition will take place through a Company's subsidiary.

ii) Market research and Customer Analytics (MR&CA) operations from Caterpillar Inc., USA (CAT) including the related Intellectual Property. The proposed acquisition is for a consideration of Rs~. 239.16 crores (equivalent in US$ million) comprising of initial and deferred considerations.

iii) the remaining 50% equity held by CA Inc. in its joint venture CA Satyam ASP Pvt. Ltd. (CA Satyam) for a total consideration of Rs 5.98 crores (equivalent US$ 1.5 million) payable in two tranches.

Info-On-Demand Sdn, the Malaysian based subsidiary of Knowledge Dynamics Pte Ltd. (the Company's subsidiary), has been formally dissolved during the last fiscal.

Joint ventures

Satyam Venture Engineering Services Pvt. Ltd., a joint venture between Satyam and Venture Global Engineering (VGE), US, earned revenue of Rs 69.73 crores and a net profit of Rs 0.45 crores for the year ended 31 March, 2008. Based on VGEs breaches of the joint venture agreement and events of default, your Company filed a Demand for Arbitration with the London Court of International Arbitration, seeking, among other things, to purchase VGEs 50% interest in SVES at the agreed upon book value price of the shares. The sole arbitrator issued an Award granting all the relief your Company sought. Your company was then successful in enforcing the Award in the US courts. During the pendency of the enforcement proceedings in the US, the suit filed by VGE challenging the Award before the district court, Secunderabad and the appeal to the High court of Andhra Pradesh respectively, were rejected. Subsequently, in a special leave petition filed by VGE, Supreme Court granted an interim stay of the share transfer portion of the Award, set aside the orders of the district court and the High court and remanded the matter back to district court to try on merits.

Social programmes

Creating value for society is an integral part of our business. Your Company believes that contributing to the well-being and development of society is an extension of everything we do. Reaffirming our role as a contributing member of social and economic environment, your Company aligns our business operations with social values. As a responsible corporate citizen, the Company leverages the power of IT to bridge the digital divide that limits opportunities for success and prosperity. As a result, we transform the lives of the underprivileged. In addition, Satyam reaches out to the society through its Corporate Social Responsibility partners, like Byrraju Foundation, for rural transformation and EMRI, for emergency management services.

Another unique public-private partnership model that was launched during the year under review was Health Management Research Institute (HMRI), in association with the Government of Andhra Pradesh and Satyam Foundation, the CSR arm of Satyam, to provide health services on call. HMRI's vision is to transform health delivery services via an easily accessible virtual platform.

During the year under review your Company contributed Rs 4.19 crores to Satyam Foundation. A report on the Corporate Social Responsibility is given elsewhere in the Annual Report.

Fixed deposits

Your Company did not accept any deposits during the year under review.

Directors

Prof M Rammohan Rao and Mr Vinod K Dham non-executive and independent directors, retire by rotation at the ensuing Annual General Meeting and are eligible for re-appointment.

Auditors

The statutory auditors M/s Price Waterhouse, Chartered Accountants, Hyderabad, retire at this Annual General Meeting. Your directors recommend their reappointment as auditors.

Conservation of Energy, Technology Absorption and Foreign Exchange earnings and outgo

The particulars as prescribed under sub-section (l)(e) of Section 217 of the Companies Act, 1956 read with Companies (Disclosure of particulars in the report of Board of Directors) Rules, 1988 forms part of this report (Annexure – A).

Employee particulars

Particulars of employees as required under Section 217(2A) of the Companies Act, 1956 and the Companies (Particulars of Employees) Rules 1975 as amended forms part of this report. However, in pursuance of Section 219(l)(b)(iv) of the Companies Act, 1956 this report is being sent to all the shareholders of the Company excluding the aforesaid information and the said particulars are made available at the registered office of the Company. The members interested in obtaining information under section 217 (2A) may write to the Company Secretary at the registered office of the Company.

Directors Responsibility Statement

As required by the provisions of Section 217 (2AA) of the Companies Act, 1956, the Directors Responsibility Statement is attached as Annexure – B.

Associate Stock Option Plans (ASOP)

As required by clause 12 of SEBI (Employee Stock Option Scheme and Employee Stock Purchase Scheme) Guidelines, 1999, the particulars of the Stock option plans of the Company are furnished as Annexure – C.

Acknowledgements

Your directors gratefully acknowledge the continued support being received from all investors, customers, vendors, banks, and other service providers as well as regulatory and government authorities in the initiatives of the Company. Your directors specially thank Associates of the Company for their focussed contributions in realising the growth strategies of the Company.

For and on behalf of
the Board of directors.

Place: Hyderabad B Ramalinga Raju
Date: 21 April 2008 Chairman

Notes

Notes to Accounts Year End: March 2008

(a) Associate Stock Option Plans

i. Scheme established prior to SEBI (Employee Stock Option Scheme and Employee Stock Purchase Scheme) Guidelines 1999 (SEBI Guidelines on Stock Options).

In May 1998, the Company established its Associate Stock Option Plan (the ASOP). The Company subsequently established an employee welfare trust called the Satyam Associates Trust (the Trust), to administer the ASOP and issued warrants to purchase 6,500,000 equity shares of Rs 2 each in the Company. In turn, the Trust periodically grants to eligible employees warrants to purchase equity shares held by trust for the issuance to the employees. The warrants may vest immediately or may vest over a period ranging from two to three years, depending on the employees length of service and performance. Upon vesting, employees have 30 days to exercise warrants. The exercise price of the warrants was fixed at Rs 450 per warrant.

At the 12th Annual General Meeting held on 28 May, 1999, shareholders approved a 1:1 Bonus issue to all shareholders as of 31 August, 1999. In order to ensure all its employees receive the benefits of the bonus issue in December 1999, the Trust exercised all its warrants to purchase the Company's shares prior to the bonus issue using the proceeds obtained from bank loans. Subsequent to this, each warrant entitles the holder to purchase 10 shares of Rs 2 each of the Company at a price of Rs 450 per warrant plus an interest component associated with the loan which the Trust assumed, for conversion of the warrants it held. The interest component is computed based on fixed vesting period and a fixed interest rate. As this scheme is established prior to the SEBI guidelines on the stock options, there is no cost relating to the grant of options under this scheme.

ii. Scheme established after SEBI Guidelines on Stock Options. Securities Exchange Board of India (SEBI) issued the Employee Stock Option Scheme and Employee Stock Purchase Scheme Guidelines 1999, which is applicable for all Stock Option Schemes established after 19 June, 1999.

The Company has established a scheme Associate Stock Option Plan – B (ASOP – B) for which 83,454,280 equity shares of Rs 2 each were earmarked. These warrants vest over a period of 2-4 years from the date of the grant. Upon vesting, associates have 5 years to exercise these shares.

Accordingly, options (net of cancellations) for a total number of 15,641,127 equity shares of Rs 2 each were outstanding as at 31 March, 2008 (2007 – 19,976,210).

iii. Associate Stock Option Plan (ADS)
The Company has established a scheme Associate Stock Option Plan (ADS) to be administered by the Administrator of the ASOP (ADS), a committee appointed by the Board of Directors of the Company. Under the scheme 5,149,330 ADS are reserved to be issued to eligible associates with the intention to issue the warrants at a price per option which is not less than 90% of the value of one ADS as reported on NYSE on the date of grant converted into Indian Rupees at the rate of exchange prevalent on the day of grant as decided by the Administrator of the ASOP (ADS). Each ADS represents two equity shares of Rs 2 each fully paid up. These warrants vest over a period of 1-10 years from the date of the grant. The time available to exercise the warrants upon vesting is as decided by the Administrator of the ASOP (ADS).

Accordingly, options (net of cancellation) for a total number of 1,283,118 ADS (2007 – 1,461,064) representing 2,566,236 equity shares of Rs 2 each were outstanding as at 31 March, 2008 (2007 – 2,922,128).

iv. Associate Stock Option Plan - Restricted Stock Units (ASOP – RSUs)
The Company has established a scheme Associate Stock Option Plan – Restricted Stock Units (ASOP – RSUs) to be administered by the Administrator of the ASOP – RSUs, a committee appointed by the Board of Directors of the Company. Under the scheme 13,000,000 equity shares are reserved to be issued to eligible associates at a price to be determined by the Administrator which shall

not be less than the face value of the share. These RSUs vest over a period of 1-4 years from the date of the grant. The maximum time available to exercise the warrants upon vesting is five years from the date of vesting.

v. Associate Stock Option Plan – RSUs (ADS) [ASOP – RSUs (ADS)]
The Company has established a scheme Associate Stock Option Plan – RSUs (ADS) to be administered by the Administrator of the ASOP – RSUs (ADS), a committee appointed by the Board of Directors of the Company. Under the scheme 13,000,000 equity shares minus the number of shares issued from time to time under the Associate Stock Option Plan – RSUs are reserved to be issued to eligible associates at a price to be determined by the Administrator not less than the face value of the share. These RSUs vest over a period of 1-4 years from the date of the grant. The maximum time available to exercise the warrants upon vesting is five years from the date of vesting.

(b) Share application money pending allotment

Amount received from associates on exercise of stock options, pending allotment of shares is shown as share application money, pending allotment.

(c) Secured Loans

Vehicles are hypothecated to the Banks as security for the amounts borrowed.

(d) Investments

i) During May 2005, the Company acquired Citisoft Plc (Citisoft), a specialist business and systems consulting firm located in the United Kingdom that has focused on the investment management industry, with operating presence in London, Boston and New York.

The Company acquired 75% of the shareholding in Citisoft for an initial cash consideration of Rs 62.35 crores (inclusive of acquisition costs), a deferred consideration of Rs 13.63 crores (equivalent GBP 1.75 million). The company was also required to pay a maximum earn-out consideration amounting to Rs 18.35 crores (equivalent GBP 2.25 million) based on achievement of targeted revenues and profits and Employee Benefit Trust (EBT) contribution of Rs 8.00 crores (equivalent GBP 0.9 million).

On 29 June, 2006, the Company acquired the remaining 25% shareholding for a consideration of Rs 27.47 crores (equivalent GBP 3.26 million) and a maximum earn-out consideration of Rs 28.87 crores (equivalent GBP 3.54 million) based on achievement of targeted revenues and profits and a maximum EBT contribution of Rs 14.68 crores (equivalent GBP 1.80 million) contingent on Citisoft achieving certain revenue and profit performance targets. The Company paid Rs 0.65 crore (equivalent GBP 0.08 million) towards EBT contribution in May 2007.

On 29 June, 2007, the Company entered into an amendment agreement with the selling shareholders providing for an early exit of the selling shareholders. As per the amendment agreement, an exit consideration of Rs 14.25 crores (equivalent GBP 1.74 million) and payment towards EBT of Rs 0.65 crores (equivalent GBP 0.08 million) is payable by the Company in July 2007 upon selling share-holders agreeing for removal of provisions of deferred consideration, maximum earn-out consideration and a portion of payments towards EBT. The exit consideration and EBT contribution payable as per the amended agreement have been paid in July 2007 and the payment has been recognised as cost of investment by the Company.

ii) During October 2005, the Company acquired Knowledge Dynamics Pte Ltd (KDPL), a leading Data Warehousing and Business Intelligence Solution provider, with operating presence in Singapore, Malaysia, USA and India.

The Company acquired 100% of the shareholding in KDPL for a consideration of Rs 14.64 crores (inclusive of acquisition costs). A maximum earn out consideration of Rs 4.87 crores (Equivalent SGD 1.84 million) is payable on 30 April, 2008, based on achievement of targeted revenues and profits.

On 19 July, 2007, the company entered into an amendment agreement with the selling shareholders of KDPL on agreeing to the terms of the agreement including removal of provisions relating to earn out consideration. As per the amendment agreement, an exit consideration of Rs 2.97 crores (Equivalent SGD 1.11 million) has been paid by the company in July 2007. In addition to the exit consideration the company agreed to make a deferred payment of Rs 0.99 crores (Equivalent SGD 0.37 million) payable by 15 May, 2008. The exit consideration and deferred payment has been recognised as cost of investment by the Company.

Further the Company agreed to make a maximum earn-out payment of Rs 2.14 crores (Equivalent SGD 0.74 million) on or before 15 May, 2008. The actual amount of earn-out payment to be made is based on the revenue of KDPL for the year 2007-08.

iii) Satyam BPO Limited (formerly known as Nipuna Services Ltd.) (Satyam BPO) issued 45,669,999 and 45,340,000 0.05% Convertible Redeemable Cumulative Preference Shares of par value of Rs 10 each fully paid-up in October

2003 and June 2004 respectively to Olympus BPO Holdings Ltd. and Intel Capital Corporation (Preference shareholders) for an aggregate consideration of Rs 91.01 crores (equivalent to US$ 20 millions). These Preference shares are to be mandatorily converted into such number of equity shares latest by June 2007 or redeemed based on certain provisions in the agreement entered with the preference shareholders relating to revenues and profits earned up to 31 March, 2006. The said preference shares, if not converted or early converted at the option of the preference shareholders based on certain triggering events, are redeemable on maturity in June 2007 at a redemption premium, which could range in between 7.5% to 13.5% p.a.

On 20 November, 2006, a Share Purchase, Redemption and Amendment Agreement (SPRA Agreement) was entered into between the Company, the preference shareholders and Satyam BPO. Out of the total preference shares, 50% of the preference shares of Rs 45.51 crores (Equivalent US$ 10 million) were redeemable for Rs 60.10 crores (Equivalent US$ 13.6 million) at the target date on 21 May, 2007 and the balance 50% were to be converted into equity shares of Satyam BPO based on the terms of the subscription agreement. The preference shareholders gave Satyam BPO a Notice of Conversion of Preference Shares and in January 2007, 45,505,000 preference shares have been converted into 6,422,267 equity shares of Satyam BPO.

Further as per the SPRA Agreement, the Company agreed to purchase and the preference shareholders agreed to sell these equity shares at an aggregate purchase price based on a formula. If the share purchase closing occurred on or before the share purchase target date (21 May, 2007) then the purchase price would range from a minimum of

Rs 152.57 crores (Equivalent US$ 35 million) to maximum of Rs 196.16 crores (Equivalent US$ 45 million), however if an acceleration event occurred the purchase price would equal Rs 196.16 crores (Equivalent US million). If the share purchase closing occurred after the share purchase target date then the purchase price shall not been less than Rs 152.57 crores (Equivalent US$ 35 million) however if an acceleration event occurred the purchase price shall not been less than Rs 196,16 crores (Equivalent US$ million). This was subject to fulfilment of terms and conditions specified in the agreement and obtaining necessary approvals from appropriate authorities. As of 31 March, 2007, an acceleration event had occurred. On 27 July, 2007 the Company has agreed to pay additional consideration of US$ 1.5 million to the preference shareholders if the share purchase closing occurs after 7 August, 2007.

On 14 August, 2007, the Company purchased 4,816,750 equity shares of Satyam BPO from Olympus BPO Holdings Ltd for Rs 141.81 crores (Equivalent US$ 88 million).

On 14 August, 2007, the Company subscribed to further 8,055,000 equity shares of Satyam BPO of Rs 10 each at a premium of Rs 60 per share aggregating to Rs 56.39 crores.

The Company also purchased 286,952 equity shares vested and exercised by Satyam BPO employees under the Employee Stock Options plan for Rs 8.47 crores as consideration for the transaction.

On 31 December, 2007, the Company purchased 1,605,617 equity shares of Satyam BPO from Intel Capital (Cayman) Corporation for Rs 45.94 crores (equivalent US$ 0.62 million).

The Company has purchased 72,000 equity shares vested and exercised by Satyam BPO employee under the

Employee Stock Options plan for Rs 2.08 crores as consideration for the transaction.

iv) On 23 October, 2007, the Company announced its intention to acquire 100% of the shares of NITOR Global Solutions Ltd, United Kingdom (Nitor), a Company specialised in the Infrastructure Management Services (IMS) space. The total consideration for this acquisition is approximately Rs 22.40 crores (equivalent GBP 2.76 million) including a performance-based payment of up to Rs 10.34 crores (Equivalent GBP 1.3 million) over two years conditional upon specified revenue and profit targets being met.

The Company has paid initial consideration of Rs 12.06 crores (equivalent GBP 1.46 million) on 4 January, 2008.

v) On 21 January, 2008, the Company announced its intention of acquiring 100% of the shares of Bridge Strategy Group LLC, (Bridge) a Chicago based strategy and general management consulting firm for a total consideration of Rs 139.51 crores (equivalent US.0 million) comprising of initial consideration, deferred consideration (non-contingent) and a contingent consideration. The transaction has not consummated as on 31 March, 2008.

(e) Land

The Company acquired 14.93 acres of land at Hyderabad from Andhra Pradesh Industrial Infrastructure Corporation (APIIC) at a rebate for an aggregate purchase consideration of Rs 7.21 crores. Non compliance with certain terms and conditions would attract withdrawal of rebate, which may increase the cost of land.

(k) Commitments and Contingencies

I. Bank Guarantees outstanding Rs 102.50 crores (2007 – Rs 98.56 crores).

II. Contracts pending execution on capital accounts, net of advances, Rs 400.65 crores (2007 – Rs 158.07 crores).

III. Forward & Option Contracts outstanding Rs 4,534.46 crores (equivalent US$ 1,133.07 millions) (2007 – Rs 1,978.98 crores (equivalent US$ 452.63 millions)} Gain/(Loss) on foreign exchange forward and options contracts which are included under the head Gain/(Loss) on exchange fluctuation in the profit and loss account amounted to Rs 38.27 crores (2007 – Rs 26.64 crores). There are no un-hedged forex exposures.

IV. Claims against the Company not acknowledged as debts – Income tax and Sales tax matters under dispute – Rs 27.98 crores (2007 – Rs 22.03 crores).

V. Contingent consideration payable in respect of acquired subsidiary companies Rs 12.36 crores (2007 – Rs 75.65 crores).

VI. Purchase commitments in respect of subsidiary. (Refer note d (v) of Schedule 15).

VII. The Company has given a corporate guarantee on behalf of a subsidiary for the loan obtained amounting to a maximum of Rs 194.65 crores (2007 – Rs 87.18 crores).

VIII. The Company entered into a joint venture agreement with Venture Global Engineering LLC (VGE) to form Satyam Venture Engineering Services Pvt. Ltd (SVES) in India. As a result of VGEs breach of the agreement between the parties, the Company filed a request for arbitration, naming VGE as respondent, with the London Court of International Arbitration (LCIA), seeking, among other things, to purchase VGEs 50% interest in SVES at the agreed upon book value price of the shares. The LCIA Arbitrator issued an Award on 3 April, 2006 in favour of the Company which it successfully enforced in the United States District Court in Michigan. During the enforcement proceedings in the US, VGE filed a petition challenging the Award before the District Court, Secunderabad and made an appeal to the High Court of Andhra Pradesh, both of which were rejected. Subsequently, in a special leave petition filed by VGE, the Supreme Court of India set aside the orders of the District Court and the High Court and granted an interim stay of the share transfer portion of the Award. The matter has been remanded back to the District Court, Secunderabad for trial on merits. The Company believes that this will not have an adverse effect on results of operations, financial condition and cash flows.

(m) Provision for Leave encashment

Effective 1 April, 2006, the Company has adopted the revised accounting standard (AS-15) Employee Benefits. Pursuant to the adoption, the transitional obligations of the Company towards leave encashment amounted to Rs 26.33 crores. As required by the standard, an amount of Rs 17.47 crores (net of related deferred tax of Rs 8.86 crores) has been adjusted against opening balance of general reserve as at 1 April, 2006.

(n) Share Premium

Share premium received during the year in schedule 2 includes Rs 16.79 crores being the Fringe Benefit Tax realised on exercise of Employees Stock Options by the associates. Also the amount paid towards Fringe Benefit Tax is disclosed in the share premium as utilised during the year.

(o) Subsequent event

i) S&V Management consulting:

On 21 April, 2008, Company announced its intention of acquiring S&V Management Consultants (S&V) a Belgium based SCM Strategy consulting firm for a total consideration of Rs 141.50 crores (equivalent US$ 35.5 million) comprising of an up-front, deferred guaranteed and deferred retention payments.

ii) Computer Associates 50% stake in CA-Satyam) V:
On 21 April, 2008, Company announced its intention of acquiring remaining 50% equity held by CA Inc in its joint venture CA Satyam ASP Pvt. Ltd. (CA Satyam) for a total consideration of Rs 5.98 crores (equivalent US$ 1.5 million) payable in two tranches.

iii) Caterpillars business division:
On 21 April, 2008, Company announced its intention to acquire the Market research and Customer Analytics (MR&CA) business unit from Caterpillar Inc., USA (CAT) including the related Intellectual Property which consists of software, processes and know-how. The proposed acquisition is for a consideration of Rs 239.16 crores (equivalent US$ 60 million) comprising of initial and deferred consideration.

(r) Dividends remitted in foreign currency

The Company does not make any direct remittances of dividends in foreign currency. The Company remits equivalent of the dividend payable to the holders of ADS in Indian Rupees to the depository bank, which is the registered shareholder on records for all owners of the Company's ADS. The depository bank purchases the foreign currencies and remits dividend to the ADS holders. The Company remitted Rs 45.61 crores during the year 2008 (2007 – Rs 45.35 crores).

(s) Reclassification

Figures for the corresponding previous year have been regrouped, recast and rearranged to conform to those of the current year wherever necessary.

CHAPTER III

Facts vs Fiction

It is said that a corporate balance sheet is like a woman's dress. It hides more than it reveals. The only thing it is sure to reveal is the management's business perspective. A company does not 'make' profit or loss. Instead, in accountant's language, it 'shows' profit or loss.

The payment of dividend to ordinary shareholders is not always linked with a company's profitability. A company may continue to pay good dividend to its shareholders even in a bad year showing lower profits by drawing from general reserve, which is also known as shareholders' fund. The lower the equity base, the easier it is for the corporate management to service the shareholders.

Corporate balance sheets also reflect the management perspective on not so much on present or past performance as future business prospects. Accounts are to be read carefully along with auditor's report, directors' report and chairman's statement to understand the real status and the present and future health of a company – the challenges it faces or likely to face, how they are to be tackled, future opportunities and management plans to exploit them for the benefit of the company and its shareholders.

Books of corporate accounts rarely expose the perfect financial picture of a company. Numbers are corruptible and often manipulated for short-term adjustments. At Satyam Computers, clearly an extreme case, the accounts book hardly represented the truth. It was all fiction, full of concocted figures. It was another matter that PwC failed to notice it. *Satyam* means Truth. But, Satyam Computers' financial accounts were full of certified lies or a travesty of truth.

It seems Satyam had been cooking up its books of accounts from the very beginning although information available on its faulty bookkeeping is from 2000-01 onwards, when its balance sheet showed Rs 141.55 crores as cash balance in current accounts and FDRs (fixed deposit receipts). Of this cash balance, Rs 140.82 crores were in current accounts. Only Rs 72.54 lakhs were in FDRs. However, the fact was that the company had only Rs 27.71 crores as actual cash and bank balances. The rest were all fiction. At the end of the second quarter (30 September) of the fiscal year 2008-09, Satyam's cash and bank balances in its books of accounts aggregated to Rs 5,160.34 crores, including Rs 3,319.17 crores in FDRs, although in reality the company had only Rs 139.78 crores as cash and bank balance.

In corporate management, it is common knowledge that too much cash and bank balance in the books of accounts of a company indicates poor financial management unless it is built for a purpose, such as maintaining a war chest to acquire a rival or to take over new businesses (M&As). On paper, Satyam was adding on an average Rs 500 crores to its cash and bank balance per year for eight years in a row. Large piles of idle cash reserves with a company also make it a potential target of take-over by others. The promoters of Satyam Computers had a very low stake in the company, especially towards the end of 2008. How was it that such financial entries (cash deposits) in the Satyam books never attracted an iota of attention of Price Waterhouse and did not induce them to do the simplest thing under the circumstance – to physically verify the statements with Satyam's bankers? Auditors are expected to do this exercise anyway as a routine matter to ascertain the factual position about such deposits and cash reserves.

Satyam maintained accounts with as many as 15 banks, including four foreign banks. Initially, these banks were Citi, HSBC, BNP Paribas, Bank of Nova Scotia, State Bank of India, Bank of Baroda, ICICI Bank, HDFC Bank, Vijaya Bank, Global Trust Bank (liquidated since),

Allahabad Bank, Indian Bank, State Bank of Travancore, Canara Bank and Times Bank (later merged). A little effort by the statutory auditors to verify with these banks would have revealed a whopping gap of Rs 5,020.55 crores between the Satyam balance sheet claim of its cash reserves at the end of 30 September 2008 and the true status of such reserves as of that day.

Similarly, verification by Price Waterhouse of such financial statements in the balance sheets in the previous years would have exposed the likewise false and inflated entries. For instance, Satyam's 2008 second quarter (July-September) financial results showed a current account balance with the New York branch of Bank of Baroda at Rs 1,784.66 crores as against the company's factual position of entire cash and balances standing at only Rs 61.71 crores at the end of the period.

CBI investigators alleged that Ramalinga Raju and his accomplices at Satyam "prepared forged fixed deposit receipts (FDRs) of various scheduled banks and also forged the monthly bank statements to inflate the balances in the current accounts, thereby inflated the cash and bank balances in the financial statements over the years". The Satyam chairman used this method to attract customers and investors, felt the CBI sleuths.

One lie leads to another and ultimately makes a pack of lies. Satyam's inflated bank balance in FDRs with its bankers generated a huge fictitious interest income year after year, which in turn inflated its cash reserves. The gross interest accrual from these fixed deposits shown in the company's accounts book at the end of the second quarter of the fiscal year 2008-09 was Rs 375.53 crores. The amount was about 536 times more than the true interest income from Satyam's FDRs from banks of a meagre amount of Rs 7.43 lakhs at the end of this period. The non-existent amount was Rs 375.46 crores.

All these entries were supposed to have been examined and certified as 'true and fair' by the company's global audit firm Price Waterhouse. These false statements escaped the scrutiny of all the concerned inspection agencies and regulatory bodies such as the government's revenue department, SEBI, the US Securities and Exchange Commission (SEC), National Stock Exchange (NSE) of India, Bombay Stock

Exchange and NYSE, and also of some of the local and global credit rating agencies presumably because they had full faith in the audit firm's professional capability and integrity. Interestingly, even the so-called hawkeyed financial and market analysts did not ask the company or themselves why Satyam was sitting on a US$ 1.4-billion cash pile.

Ramalinga Raju had confessed that the balance sheet as of 30 September 2008 carried an accrued interest of Rs 376 crores, which did not actually exist. At no point of time, Satyam's interest accrual from FDRs exceeded Rs 5 crores in a single year. The average annual interest accrual of Satyam Computers in the last 10 years of the company under Ramalinga Raju was less than Rs 1 crore.

How did Satyam handle the payment of 'tax deducted at source' (TDS) on the inflated interest income on the company's books of account? Under the Income Tax Act of the Government of India (Section 194 A) tax is required to be deducted at source on interest paid/credited on accrual/payment basis. Accordingly, Satyam Computers' balance sheet, certified by its directors and auditors, made a TDS payment of Rs 169.50 crores for the first quarter (April-June) of 2008-09 and Rs 30.50 crores for the second quarter of that year to the income-tax (I-T) department. However, the actual TDS payments made to the department for the two quarters were Rs 5.54 lakhs and Rs 1.53 lakhs, respectably.

How could Satyam Computers generate such large cash surpluses year after year unless it had a really impressive bottom line, part of which was retained by the company after payment of dividends to shareholders? The large retained profits are mainly used for investments to earn revenue for shareholders. Bank FDRs are one such avenue for investment. It is the safest and the easiest and most conservative of all investment options. Corporate bottom line is linked with its top line. It is also linked with efficient use of capital.

Satyam Computers had produced one of the best top lines in the industry. It was the fourth largest revenue earner in the IT industry. Going by its director's report for the year ended 31 March 2008, Satyam's income from software services was Rs 8,137 crores as against Rs 6,228 crores in the previous year (2006-07). The company's post-tax profit was Rs 1,716 crores as against Rs 1,423 crores in 2006-07. It paid 175 per cent dividend to its ordinary shareholders, the same as in the previous year. Its share capital was only Rs 134 crores. The only real or the truthful part of the financial statement was the dividend part since the cash out-go was small and manageable. The rest of the items in the financial statement were all fudged with Price Waterhouse standing by those bogus numbers. The top line was inflated by raising false invoices through illegal means.

Satyam's fund mismanagement story is not any different from many other such Indian joint stock companies which fell victim to the personal greed of their promoter-managers with their auditors playing a rather supportive role by not providing a 'true and fair' view of the state of affairs of those companies to their stakeholders. The Satyam chairman's sudden confession of the fudged accounts brought down the company's share price to Rs 35 each at some stage. Satyam Computers' operations included software development, consulting, system design, system integration and application maintenance. The services were all fee-based. Bills were raised on 'Time and Material' or on 'Fixed Bid' basis. Time spent on an assignment by associates or employees is billed on hourly basis or on daily/monthly basis. A Fixed Bid project is billed on delivery of the agreed output.

The standard industry practice is that a software company's sales team interacts with the customer to understand the requirements. Its technical team ascertains the efforts needed for the delivery to negotiate the contract on payment terms and billing on Time and Material or Fixed Bid basis. Once a contract is signed, the customer issues purchase order to the service provider detailing technical requirements and commercial aspects, including when and how to bill/invoice the customer. Invoice is a demand note for payment against services rendered. The amount mentioned in an invoice is shown as 'Receivables' in the service provider's books of accounts. The name 'Debtor' is used alternatively. Once the payment is received, it is reconciled as 'Cash in Hand'.

Ramalinga Raju's confession mentioned an overstated debtor's position of Rs 490 crores (as against Rs 2,651 crore reflected in the books). Satyam had developed several in-house applications and a network of systems by integrating those applications for the generation of invoices.

A typical invoice contained customer's name, project ID, project name, purchase order, details of the amount payable, etc. The invoices were exported to the Oracle Financials. For emergency generation of invoices, a separate technique called 'EXCELL – PORTING' was used and access to this was given to only a chosen group of associates who formed part of the Accounts Receivable (AR) Team.

Modern accounting involves more number of IT professionals than traditional accountants. Even the accountants possess deep knowledge of the application of IT. Global audit firms such as PwC, KPMG, Ernst & Young and Deloitte are all technology-savvy and employ large number of software professionals for the purpose of accounting and development of techniques.

The Price Waterhouse audit team was fully conversant with the billing and accounting techniques followed by Satyam, its invoice management system (IMS), Satyam Projects Repository (SPR), etc. The official investigation revealed that between 1 April 2003 and 31 December 2008, "a total of 74,625 invoices were generated in IMS through the EXCEL-PORTING technique". Of these invoices, some were earmarked 'H' to identify the 'invoice field status'. Of the 4,625 invoices, the invoice field status of 7,561 were marked 'S'. The latter were "hidden from the view of Finance In-charges (FICs)". And, 6,603 of them "were found in the Oracle Financials reflecting the actual sales. The total amount shown against these 7,561 invoices is Rs 5,117.69 crores and those corresponding to the 6,603 found in Oracle Financials were Rs 4,746 crores. Several validations were conducted with regard to the genuineness of these 7,561 invoices and it was confirmed that "they were all false". The customers referred to in these invoices said they never received them. In Oracle Financials, the payments were shown to have been received at the Satyam account with the New York branch of Bank of Baroda, which denied the receipt of any such payment. Out of 33,510 associates shown to have been connected with the project IDs mentioned in these invoices, as many as 32,761 names were not actually involved or allocated with the task. Some 205 project IDs, which were used in preparing those false invoices, did not exist in the SPR.

The bogus invoices bolstered Satyam's income from software services. When the company's top line itself was fudged in this fashion on a sustained basis, one could imagine the kind of impact it would carry on the rest of the balance sheet entries and, finally, on the bottom line. In 18 quarterly accounts between April-June 2004 and July-September 2008, the Satyam Computers sales were inflated to the tune of Rs 4,257 crores. The management information systems (MIS) generated every quarter established the existence of two sets of sales data, one real and the other falsely inflated. Several such sets of actual and inflated MIS data sheets were retrieved from a server in the course of the official investigation that clearly showed the organised manner in which the financial conspiracy was hatched and carried out over a period of time. The gap between the actual sales and falsely inflated sales income in the last eight quarterly accounts (till July-September 2008) was palpably abnormal. However, this did not raise any suspicion in the minds of Satyam's dutiful auditors.

The biggest single head of investment of most computer software companies is under 'human resources'. Employees are the biggest asset and strength of any software company. They generate income for their employers. Their strength indicates the top line as well as the health of a software company. Satyam Computers had on paper some 53,000 employees to contribute to its top line. The 'loading factor' is key to the business success of any software company. It implies the actual percentage of employees on the rolls of a company who are engaged in revenue generating projects. The employees are categorised into two groups – offshore category and onsite category. Those working in India are bunched under the offshore category and those working at customer's premises abroad belong to the onsite category. The loading factor percentages for both the categories are published by the company on a quarterly basis. Higher loading factor indicates higher percentage of employees in revenue generating projects. Not only does it provide confidence to existing customers in the company's capability, but also attracts new customers and helps market the company's products (services).

As the company's fudged financials proved, Satyam Computers was a master in doctoring both the number of employees and the loading factor. After the confessional statement of Ramalinga Raju and the subsequent collapse of the company, it was estimated that the actual employees' strength of Satyam Computers was around 45,000 only. The company's employment register was said to have carried an inflated strength in order to inflate the company's revenue. What is more, the company maintained a huge under-utilised strength at high cost putting additional burden on its resources.

On paper, Satyam Computers claimed an average 74.88 per cent 'investor-link' loading factor in the offshore category between 2006 and 2008. The actual 'head count' loading factor was only 62.02 per cent. Similarly, the same in the onsite category was shown as 96.76 per cent whereas the actual number was 94.86 per cent. The investigation revealed that Satyam's bench strength was as high as 40 per cent in the offshore category during this period, giving deceptive information to investors and customers on the company's performance. For instance, based on these exaggerated claims, Satyam's Q2 (July-September) 2008, revenue was shown as Rs 2,700 crores whereas the actual figure was Rs 2,112 crores. The operating margin was given as Rs 649.27 crore (24 per cent of the revenue) as against the factual margin of only Rs 61 crores (three per cent of the revenue). The distortion of the revenue income led to an artificial rise in cash and bank balances by Rs 588 crores in Q2 alone.

Auditors are often said to be the eyes and ears of shareholders as well as stakeholders of any company. They play possibly the most important role to ensure corporate governance. Particularly in a society where the corporate sector is mostly family managed and joint stock companies are run by business families often with very small holding, statutory auditors are expected to play a very positive role in preventing insider trading, siphoning-off of corporate funds, diversion of funds, etc by promoter-managers.

Hundreds of large and medium-sized companies failed in the 1960s and 1970s, turned sick and were forced to close down without advance warning partly due to the nexus between their promoter-managers and auditors. Few ordinary shareholders outside the entrepreneur-manager families had any clue until these companies collapsed. The auditors' reports of these companies did not reflect 'true and fair' view of the state of affairs of those companies until they reached the point of no return. The auditors were hand-in-glove with the management. Their reports failed to raise timely alarm for the benefit of the shareholders, creditors and suppliers. While the companies turned sick, their promoters prospered in other businesses. The promoters had already siphoned out enough funds to try their luck in other businesses. Only innocent shareholders, banks and financial institutions, sundry creditors and suppliers suffered the losses.

A government report in the early 1980s had estimated the combined loss of commercial banks in India on account of corporate bad debts at over Rs 2,40,000 crores, which was equivalent to US$ 300 billion at the then existing exchange rate of eight Indian rupees for a dollar. As late as in the 1990s, few knew about the true picture of the erstwhile automotive tyre giant Dunlop India's financial heath before its imminent closure under the then entrepreneur-manager, M R Chhabria. Price Waterhouse, which was one of Dunlop's two statutory auditors, gave up the company's accounts rather too late to be of any good use to either the company's majority non-family shareholders or its bankers The promoters had, by then, taken out a lot of funds and, in the process, inflicted a loss of Rs 959 crores (around US$ 200 million) on a single institutional investor, LIC, India's largest life insurance company owned by the government.

To begin with, Satyam Computers had eleven promoters. Ten of them belonged to the B Ramalinga Raju family, comprising his father, mother, brothers, their wives, and a private family concern, Satyam

Construction Company. These promoters together held 34,89,400 shares, representing only 18.78 per cent of the total number of ordinary shares of the company in 1992. On 31 May 1995, the Ramalinga Raju family floated five investment companies to sell their shares in Satyam Computers to these privately operated share-trading firms. The names of those investment companies were: Elem Investments, High Grace Investments, Fincity Investments, High Sound Investments (name changed later to SNR Investments) and VEEYES Investments Private Limited. In 1997, B Ramalinga Raju's two sons, B Rama Raju Jr and B Teja Raju, also became corporate promoters.

Following an issue of bonus shares by Satyam Computers in 1999, the Raju family's total stock holding in the company increased by 44,18,602 shares to 89,30,606 shares. However, this brought down the family stake in the company by more than one per cent to 17.34 per cent of the expanded share capital. The same year, three of the Raju family members, B Suryanarayana Raju, Mrs B Jhansi Rani and Mrs Appalanarasamma, off-loaded their shares in Satyam Computers indirectly through the accounts of some 17 individuals, known to be highly trusted employees and their family members.

These persons, in turn, deposited the shares in their DEMAT accounts and sold those shares in the market through the five Raju family investment companies. The investment companies, then, sold those shares in the market and the sale proceeds were transferred to the individual accounts of those 17 persons. The latter transferred the amount back to their original owners, the three Raju family members, through cheques. The cumbersome sale and share transfers within the Raju family were believed to avoid the charges of insider trading and the possible glare of the regulatory authority.

The promoters of Satyam Computers had, over the years, sold large number of shares in the open market and received huge amounts. The share prices were rigged. The company's forged annual balance sheet and profit and loss account, audited and certified by Price Waterhouse, helped boost the share prices over the years. Over a period of time, nine of the Raju family members, including the Satyam Computers chairman, and Maytas Infrastructure, earned Rs 707 crores from 'timely' off-loading of some of their holdings in the IT company. In addition, one of the family investment companies made Rs 8.14 crores through 'timely' sale of Satyam Computers' high priced shares. High prices of Satyam Computers shares in the bourses and attractive earnings per share (EPS), all based on the company's cooked up accounts books, helped the Raju family make enormous money by way of both stock sale and annual dividends. The Satyam promoters grossed a dividend income of over Rs 115 crores between 1994 and 2008.

Thanks to the systematic sale of the promoters' shares in Satyam Computers, without drawing any serious attention of either the auditors or the institutional shareholders and analysts, the family holding fell to only 8.59 per cent in 2006, the year when the company management made another bonus issue to give Raju & family another bunch of 2,78,67,000 shares. By 31 December 2008, the Raju family's stake in Satyam Computers nosedived to 1.87 per cent as it adopted a very innovative route to raise money from the market by mortgaging the family's share assets. In 2006, B Ramalinga Raju promoted another private company, SRSR Holdings, with his brothers B Suryanarayana Raju and B Rama Raju and son B Teja Raju as directors. On 14 September 2006, all the shares of Satyam Computers held in the accounts of B Ramalinga Raju, his wife Nandini Raju, brother B Rama Raju and brother's wife B Radha Raju were transferred to SRSR Holdings.

Altogether, the Satyam Computers promoters had floated as many as 327 companies, incorporated between 1999 and 2008. They were located at 12 addresses. SRSR Holdings were used to raise personal loans from non-banking financial companies (NBFCs) by pledging shares as collateral security with them. SRSR Holdings helped its members raise Rs 1,744.36 crores from half a dozen NBFCs which included such big names as Deutsche Investments India, GE Capital, DSP Merryll Lynch, Deutsche Mutual Fund and Sicom.

The audit firm, Price Waterhouse, and its learned partners may have nothing much to do with Ramalinga Raju's or other Satyam Computers promoters' private share transaction deals, their setting up of hundreds of shell companies ostensibly to facilitate scores of land deals, raising private loans and their reinvestment in the IT company without proper documentation. But can it prove its innocence for completely overlooking the concocted entries in the accounts book which worked as the fountainhead of all corruptions and malpractices by the company's promoters?

CHAPTER IV

The Pricetag

It may be just a matter of coincidence that the fudging of accounts at Satyam Computers started with the appointment of the Indian arm, Price Waterhouse, of the world's largest audit and financial accountancy firm –PricewaterhouseCoopers, after the merger of Coopers & Lybrand – as the IT company's statutory auditors. Or, was it part of a well-hatched conspiracy between the auditors and the client to systematically cook up the company's accounts books in the following years?

Price Waterhouse is one of the few foreign names registered with the Institute of Chartered Accountants of India (ICAI), the self-regulatory body of the industry, for historical reasons. ICAI does not allow registration of foreign names. No foreign direct investment (FDI) is allowed in the audit and accountancy business in India. Since Price Waterhouse, a pioneer in the financial audit business in India, existed long before the creation of ICAI through an Act of Parliament, it was allowed to retain the foreign name tag and remain networked with the global body. A few other early audit firms with foreign names were also allowed to practice under their foreign nametags.

Price Waterhouse maintained a big professional image over decades despite its occasional battering due to controversies over the integrity of partners. None of these controversies matched the magnitude and scale of the firm's role in Satyam Computers' accounts jugglery. It would appear that Ramalinga Raju had not only chosen the audit firm to conduct Satyam's statutory audit, but also influenced the selection and work ethics of audit partners. Like all key officials at Satyam, they too spoke Raju's mother tongue, Telegu. One of the Satyam Computers audit partners, S Gopalakrishnan, was earlier accused of negligence in auditing the books of accounts of Hyderabad-based Global Trust Bank (GTB), a joint-stock banking company, which collapsed in 2003 under the burden of huge non-performing assets (NPAs). Gopalakrishnan was one of the three auditors, belonging to the audit firm Lovelock & Lewes, charged with the failure to detect the bank's huge levels of NPAs.

The other two auditors, P Ramakrishna and Manish Aggrawal, had been earlier booked by ICAI and found guilty of 'professional misconduct'. Lovelock & Lewes is a Price Waterhouse network firm. Interestingly, Gopalakrishnan saw himself elevated later as the partner in charge of Price Waterhouse, Hyderabad. While Manish Aggrawal left the audit firm, Ramakrishna was still with Lovelock & Lewes when the ICAI central committee upheld the findings of professional misconduct of its disciplinary committee during early 2010 in the GTB case. Strange are the ways of these audit firms, always taking shelter under the veil of professional secrecy. The nature and the extent of 'misconduct' by those audit partners were never made public.

CBI investigations reveal some very interesting information involving Gopalakrisnnan and Raju's Satyam Computers. The company's financial statements carried the signature of Gopalakrishnan as partner of Price Waterhouse (PW), its statutory auditors since the financial year 2000-01. The company started cooking up its books of accounts in a very systematic manner from the same year. ICAI records showed Gopalakrishnan as partner of Price Waterhouse, Bangalore branch, and not the apex India firm, also called Price Waterhouse. This may appear to be contrary to the established procedure and said to be violating the requirements of the Auditing and Assurance Standards (AAS) of ICAI under rule No. 28. These procedural lapses apart, the Price Waterhouse partner-in-charge did not seem to have done his job properly and according to the rule books to physically verify Satyam Computers' statements with regard to the company's bank balances, FDRs, investments, liabilities, sales income, key items of expenditure, taxes paid to the income-tax authorities, etc.

Even the existence of large idle bank balances on the Satyam's books of account did not prompt the auditors to follow the standard practice to write to the concerned banks to obtain confirmation of such balances and note the discrepancies, if any, recorded in the books. If the auditors met this simple AAS requirement, the Satyam Computers management's financial jugglery would have been exposed at the very first instance. Instead, Gopalakrishnan presented a very rosy picture of the company before the company's audit committee year after year and certified the compliance of financial discipline and controls by the company. Allegedly, the auditors made available computer-generated false letters to banks seeking confirmation of balances only for the purpose of creation of records.

For the first time, an 'information technology general check' (ITGC) was carried out in the company in 2006-07 by the head of Price Waterhouse's information systems audit, which detected some 135 control deficiencies. The result was communicated to the audit team with the assertion that the IT systems in existence were not fully integrated and could be subjected to manipulation. In view of this, it was suggested that the audit team should carry out a more elaborate and substantial examination of the company's financials. The information about the control deficiencies and subsequent action, if any, by the audit team as per the suggestions made by the IT systems men was never shared with the Audit Committee.

The other Price Waterhouse audit partner, Talluri Srinivas, too maintained silence on the balance sheet manipulation and non-compliance of the ICAI audit and assurance standards. The integrated audit was conducted as per the standards of the Public Company Accounting Oversight Board (PCAOB). Such audit is important to establish its impact on internal control and financial accounting. The Price Waterhouse partners, on the contrary, not only failed to bring those control deficiencies to the notice of the company's audit committee, but also seemed to ignore the warning totally to encourage the fraudulent accounting practices for unknown reasons. Also, no comment was made on those control deficiencies in the company's audit report for the year though they were substantive and material in nature.

Corporate deals always come at a cost. There is no free lunch. If Price Waterhouse and its partners, Gopalakrishnan and Talluri Srinivas, representing the firm's Bangalore establishment accepted on its face value every financial detail that the Satyam Computers management dished out in the balance sheet and the profit & loss account, it could not have been just for an ordinary fee. India's fourth ranking IT company paid much higher fees to its auditors than those paid by somewhat comparable IT firms such as Wipro and Infosys.

Even India's biggest IT firm, Tata Consultancy Services (TCS), which was three times larger than Satyam Computers in terms of sales turnover in 2006-07 and 2007-08, was no match for Satyam when it came to payment of audit fees to the company's the then auditors, S B Billimoria & Co, an associate of Deloitte Touche Tohmatsu (DTT). Billimoria had since returned the mandate. The TCS board appointed a new auditor, DHS, also a Deloitte associate. The turnover of TCS was US$ 4.29 billion (Rs 18,347 crores) in 2006-07 and US$ 5.69 billion in 2007-08 (Rs 24,467 crores). In comparison, Satyam Computers' reported sales income was only US$ 1.46 billion (Rs 5,840 crores) in 2006-07 and US$ 1.9 billion (Rs 8,170 crores) in 2007-08. Yet, Satyam paid the highest audit fees in the IT industry.

Wipro, the second largest Indian IT company having a turnover of US$ 4.52 billion (Rs 19,436 crores) in 2007-08, paid an audit fee of Rs 1.10 crores. Infosys, having a sales income of US$ 4.02 billion (Rs 17,286 crores) in 2007-08, paid only Rs 83 lakhs as audit fees. The same year, Satyam paid a whopping Rs 3.73 crores as audit fees to Price Waterhouse. In addition, the IT company paid Rs 1.27 crores to Price Waterhouse as fees for other (non-audit) services. Satyam Computers, it would appear, was extremely generous in serving dollops to the audit firm. Or, one may say, Satyam knew the price of The Price! The payment of such high audit fees by companies in India is generally unheard of. Did PwC compromise on its professional ethics for such fat fees? Can the payment of such high audit fees be treated as 'inducement' posing 'threat to compliance with fundamental principles' of accounting under the ICAI code of ethics?

The 'Big Four' world audit firms – PwC, KPMG, E&Y and DTT – are using their Indian network audit arms, brought under control through indirect means, to make big bucks on consultancy. The Indian audit firms are used for catching big-ticket clients for them. For instance, Price Waterhouse earned Rs 1.27 crores from Satyam alone in 2007-08 on account of 'non-audit' services. PwC's gross consultancy income from Indian clients for the year could run into several billions of rupees.

According to ICAI, the Big Four are twisting and circumventing laws while providing auditing services in India. While these global firms are licensed to provide only consultancy services, they seem to be happily carrying out other services which they are not permitted to. The issue came up in the course of an ICAI investigation into the Satyam accounts. "It has been noticed that MAFs (multinational accounting firms), entered through automatic/FIPB (Foreign Investment Promotion Board) route for rendering consultancy services, are transgressing the permission so granted and are rendering taxation services, auditing, accounting and bookkeeping services and legal services", reported a high level ICAI committee, headed by its former president Uttam Prakash Agarwal. The committee further stated that "Indian firms and MAFs are de facto the same entities providing the assurance, management and related services and as such their operations are designed to circumvent the provisions of the Chartered Accountants Act, 1949, and regulations framed thereunder".

Indian laws do not permit foreign direct investment (FDI) in accounting, auditing and bookkeeping, taxation and legal services. However, these so-called foreign consultancy firms seem to be doing just that with the help of their network Indian audit and accountancy firms. PwC's Indian associates include all PW firms and Lovelock and Lewes. Deloitte's India associates are C C Chokshi, A F Ferguson, Fraser & Ross, P C Hansotia and S B Billimoria. KPMG is associated with

BSR (Bharat S Raut & Co.) firms while E&Y has tie-ups with S R Batliboi entities. In 2009, ICAI had reportedly sought details from 94 CA firms about their arrangement with the international accounting firms. Not all of them cared to furnish complete information. "The reply from some of the firms is silent as to whether any payment is being made to obtain the licence to use the brand name", the ICAI committee reported.

Going by the magnitude of financial forgery in Satyam accounts and the slow and sheepish reaction by the industry and regulatory bodies both in India and the USA, where the company is also listed and the audit firm PwC is globally headquartered, what value would society attach to the so-called code of ethics for professional accountants and corporate governance? An auditor or practicing accountant should be and, also appear to be, above such controversies which question his or his firm's integrity and objectivity. Umpteen numbers of publications are available for both students and practicing accountants across the world on accounting concepts and how corporate financial statements, scrutinised by those chartered accountants, should represent 'true and fair view' of the state of affairs of those corporate entities and their profits and losses.

Accounting norms and requirements vary from business to business. The requirement of the services sector, which includes IT, banking and insurance, finance companies, share broking, shipping and air transport, are not the same as the manufacturing sector of industry. There exist several accounting standards, such as International Financial Reporting Standards (IFRS), International Accounting Standards (IAS), and country specific Generally Accepted Accounting Principles (GAAP), international and country specific laws and regulatory bodies, to ensure good and reliable accounting practices, financial discipline and controls which are fundamental to good governance.

The Indian-originated Satyam Computers was a joint stock multinational company listed with stock exchanges both in India and the US (NYSE). The company's auditors are an associate of one of the four biggest international audit firms. Yet, it required an astounding confession by the company's chairman, B Ramalinga Raju, before the board members for the world to know how Satyam fudged its books of accounts for a period over nine years, trashing all accounting standards and principles in the face of its internal and statutory auditors, bankers, regulatory authorities in India and the US, international rating agencies and stock analysts. Even the confession did not change the profile of the auditors leave alone bearing an impact on the business operations of PwC and its associates in India or elsewhere in the world.

It was more than a year after the confession by the Satyam Chairman, and after the two Price Waterhouse audit partners were jailed on charges of complicity in the case, followed by several incomplete investigations held by regulatory authorities in India and Satyam's subsequent auction sale to another Indian IT firm Tech Mahindra, that the US Public Company Accounting Oversight Board (PCAOB) decided to impose 'sanctions' against the two Indian auditors, both affiliated with PwC, for non-cooperation. The US PCAOB is responsible for monitoring public accounting firms there. It has the authority under Sarbanes-Oxley Act, 2002, to investigate into the affairs of audit firms in the US.

The two Indian auditors, Shiva Prasad Pulavarthi and Chintapatla Ravindernath, had reportedly refused to 'cooperate' with PCAOB investigators in connection with the Satyam fraud. Both were managers on Satyam's audit function for several years and resigned from the audit firm only in January 2010. At the time of writing this book, both are believed to have submitted 'settlement offers' to the PCAOB and consented to the sanctions, without admitting or denying their role in the massive accounts jugglery that continued for years.

Neither the US PCAOB nor the Securities and Exchange Commission (SEC) seem to be attaching much priority to investigate into the accounting fraud at Satyam although many investors in the US suffered financial losses after the stock price collapsed following Raju's confession. It could be that their hands are full with more complex investigations involving bigger financial frauds in several US companies and investment banks in which investors have lost billions. The SEC had not been able to crackdown fast enough even on Bernard Madoff's missing US$ 65-billion Ponzi scheme where, as in the case of Satyam, technology was misused to maintain false records of investments and generate false statements. Also, it could be that PwC (originally UK-headquartered) is priceless for global US commerce, especially after the collapse of the audit firm Arthur Andersen. Arthur Andersen was named in the massive financial fraud at Enron, the giant American utility company of the 1990s, and the consolidation in the public accounting industry that followed. PwC, the firm, is unlikely to be pulled up in the USA by the regulators for lapses on the part of a few associate member accountants in India and the US, overlooking false book entries in the comparatively small US$ 1.4-billion Satyam accounting fraud case.

At best, the regulators may take some individual penal actions against the concerned audit partners and their underlings. It would have probably been a different story if the audit firm was a much smaller and far less influential local entity, the likes of which are generally lectured upon by regulators and mentors on issues such as fairness, integrity and good corporate governance.

Surprisingly, even in India, the public response to the country's biggest corporate financial fraud was rather low key and short lived. Raju's revelation of accounts jugglery hardly shocked business, industry, money managers, regulators, the Reserve Bank, politicians and the government in India. A much bigger and sustained noise was made over a US$ 100 million fraud at ITC Limited, an associate of BATCO of the UK. The deceit was detected through a special audit conducted by the audit firm Lovelock & Lewes at the instance of overseas investors to expose the mischief by the local management of the diversified tobacco giant in the mid-1990s. Interestingly, Lovelock & Lewes, which was also ITC's statutory auditors at that time, failed to notice the fraud in the course of their normal audit function. While several ITC directors faced the music, the audit firm was never pulled up for 'overlooking' the financial fraud at the first instance.

The CBI investigation into the Satyam case could not have been avoided despite Raju's political clout both at the state and the national levels. To minimise the scope of controversy, the government acted smartly and fast to appoint official investigators into the Satyam affair. All the main culprits, including the promoters and the company's two audit partners, were arrested. The Satyam board was quickly superseded to regain investor confidence. The company was soon put under the hammer for sale to the best bidder. However, the proceedings against the financial conspirators in the erstwhile Satyam Computers seemed to have slowed down despite the first charge sheet by the CBI within months. Raju, who reported sick, spent probably more time in a comfortable hospital cabin than in jail. He even got himself bailed out for a while before he was sent back by orders from the higher court following massive media criticism against his becoming a free man before the trial.

In all fairness to CBI, it did a good job, and very fast, compared to other more specialised agencies such as ICAI, SEBI and ED which have also been investigating into the Satyam case. Also, the government was quick to outline a corporate governance code in a new Bill, which is designed to replace the existing Companies Act, 1956. However, no serious debate on related issues such as growing promoter-auditor nexus in the corporate sector, auditors' role in corporate governance, auditors' remuneration and their involvement in more lucrative non-audit functions, the selection process and corruption of so-called independent directors from India and abroad (all Satyam independent directors, who sang to the tune of Raju and approved the company's Maytas acquisition agenda, had an Andhra link) took place within apex industry bodies such as FICCI, ASSOCHAM, CII, AMFI and ICAI and investor forums.

Industry barons, who shared platforms with Raju, maintained total silence. Some of Raju's old friends and colleagues even said, under condition of anonymity, that 'book-cooking' in IT firms is not unusual. Quipped one of Raju's friends: "Why doesn't one inspect the 2001-02 balance sheets of some of India's other top IT companies, earlier engaged in delivering Y2K solution contracts, and find out if those companies showed fall of income because of the huge sudden loss of contracts after the year 2000? Fictitious head counts and inflated billings in IT industry were certainly not a Satyam invention." They felt that if the 'conspiracy' to block the acquisition of Maytas Infra and Maytas Properties did not succeed, the world would have never known about the financial fraud at Satyam. "Raju wouldn't have made a confession then," a former senior colleague of Raju reasoned.

Subsequent to the developments at Satyam, for which many blame ICAI for being soft on big names in the profession, the apex professional body turned the heat on as many as ten large listed companies in India 'for discrepancies in financial reporting' and alerted the market regulator, SEBI, as well as the Government of India. The companies were not named considering the panic it could create in the stock market. The ten public companies, the shares of which are traded on both the Bombay Stock Exchange (BSE) and National Stock Exchange (NSE), were identified by the accounting regulator's Financial Reporting Review Board, having *suo moto* power to look into the published accounts of various companies, after it noticed discrepancies in their financial reporting. Following this, ICAI asked its disciplinary committee to find out the role of auditors in each of the cases and whether they were lax in carrying out their duties.

ICAI's action justifies the fear of a growing nexus between auditors and clients and rampant corporate accounting fraud in India. Ideally, ICAI and SEBI should work together to unearth corporate accounting fraud which is often leading to share price rigging and over pricing of IPOs. In 2010, several leading Indian telecommunications companies were alleged to fudge their accounts to cheat the government on its share of revenue.

Indian telecom companies, notorious for constantly making and changing tariff plans and so-called concessional offers and also sharing subscribers' personal data with all kinds of marketing companies for undisclosed fees, are robbing not only the ignorant public but also the government. The latest special audit reports of some of the telecom companies suggest that the industry may have robbed the government of close to Rs 1,000 crores by way of fudging or misreporting their revenue income.

The telecom industry has even challenged the authority of the government to engage the services of the Comptroller and Auditor General of India (CAG) to review the audited accounts of the telecommunications companies. The government seems to have had reasons to strongly believe that telecom companies are cooking up their books of accounts to understate income and pay less license fee and spectrum usage fee to the government according to their revenue sharing contract ingrained in the operating license agreement.

Any understatement of revenue is bound to have an impact on a company's bottom line or the taxable income as well. That means such a company is robbing the exchequer not only on payment of shared revenue, but also on payment of corporate tax, dividend payment tax etc. The suspicion gained ground after the government went through the balance sheet of R-Com (Reliance Communications) some time ago to note the discrepancy.

Special auditors appointed by the Department of Telecommunications (DoT), Government of India, last year, to examine the books of accounts of a number of telecom companies have generally found 'nothing wrong' with the statements of accounts but noticed that these companies 'failed' to add dealers' margin for selling recharge coupons as part of their revenue. And, as such the companies did not pay the license fee on the additional revenue on this account to the government. According to these reports, telecommunications company Bharti Airtel's liability on account of such under reporting of revenue was Rs 98 crores, Idea Cellular's Rs 74 crores and Vodafone Essar's Rs 188 crores. Among other major private sector players, whose additional license fee liabilities could not be fully ascertained, were Tata Teleservices, Aircel and Reliance Communications. The industry's contention was that the income from dealers' margin on coupon sales is more of a notional nature. The telecom tribunal also held the same view. And, therefore, no license fee is payable on such notional income. The government is not convinced and wants to get to the bottom of the matter by engaging CAG to look into the books of accounts and re-inspect the financial statements of all the telecom companies to ascertain the true picture of their revenue.

Not surprisingly, the government's decision to involve CAG to re-examine the accounts books has been strongly contested by the industry, which says CAG has no audit jurisdiction over privately-held companies. CAG itself thinks otherwise. The government super-auditor says a 2002 official notification authorises CAG to audit the accounts of telecommunications companies as the latter are required to share a part of the revenue with the government. Telecom companies are required to pay six to ten per cent of their annual revenue as license fee and up to six percent as spectrum usage charges. Thus, underreporting of revenue could mean substantial loss of income to the government.

Any loss of revenue to the government certainly falls under the purview of the CAG audit although the power has not yet been exercised by the government auditor. Bharti Airtel is said to have objected to the CAG review also on the ground that the nature of information being sought was confidential and sensitive from the competition point of view and falls beyond the company's obligations under the license agreement. The strongest objection to the CAG review has come from Bharti Airtel which is indirectly held by the Singapore government through its equity participation in SingTel, Bharti's single largest corporate shareholder. Will the Singapore Telecom (SingTel) management dare express a similar audacity to challenge its government's power and authority to inspect its accounts?

In America, the Government Accounting Office (GAO) and the Comptroller of the United States can order special audit of books of accounts of any joint stock company and public or private enterprise if they deem fit. No company can challenge these authorities on grounds that such an exercise may lead to the leakage of competition sensitive information or cause inconvenience and extra-financial burden for the detailed review of the books of accounts. After all, the stakeholders, including the government, have the right to ascertain the veracity of corporate accounts books when serious doubts are raised about their authenticity.

Few will agree that corporate audited accounts project the gospel truth. They only present 'fair' picture as against 'correct' picture. For long, the auditor-client nexus has been a matter of concern for lawmakers and regulatory bodies of public accountants across the world. The government has a big role to play in this regard to ensure that corporate management objectives do not run counter to government and social objectives. Unfortunately, India's economic reform has failed to ensure adherence to social responsibility, customer care and reliable presentation of financial accounts by business enterprises.

Whether a CAG review of books of accounts of telecom companies ultimately establishes any serious discrepancy or not, the government auditor cannot be prevented from doing a re-inspection job to clear its doubt about the authenticity of the numbers. Corporate audit is a constant process. For listed companies in India, it is a quarterly requirement under the listing agreement with stock exchange. The quarterly results given are internally audited. Despite that companies are known to fudge their accounts with or without the involvement of their internal auditors and statutory auditors. If Price Waterhouse could overlook false financial statements in the erstwhile Satyam Computers' books of accounts for eight consecutive years, there is no reason to believe in the efficiency and truthfulness of auditors of telecom companies or for that matter of any company. Now that the government has serious doubts about the revenue statements of telecom companies, it should go ahead with the proposed CAG review of the books of accounts of these firms at least to clear the air of thick suspicion.

The cheating on revenue-linked payment of license fees, usage charges, cess, royalty, etc. to the government by business corporations is rather common in India. The latest financial scandal involving the fudging of accounts by a host of private mining companies in the Bellary-Hospet region in South India is believed to have cost the government in excess of Rs 5,000 crores in under-recovery of collection of cess and royalties. Like those telecom companies, these private sector mining enterprises are alleged to have understated the revenue in their books of accounts to deprive the government of its rightful share of their mining income. It is disgraceful, but it is there. A lenient attitude on the part of the government towards such offences will only encourage more corporate financial corruption which is unfortunately growing in India despite various tax reforms.

In fact, not many public accountants in India found fault with the PwC or E&Y for the Satyam accounting fraud or Maytas Properties' valuation. They blame it on the 'system' and 'greed' which are universal and not unique to India. Corporate greed, incorrect financial reporting, the existence of incompetent and corrupt independent directors on company boards, absence of early warning from auditors and the laid-back attitude of overworked regulators having little full-time help have seen the fall of many large corporations and financial institutions across the globe.

Auditing is no longer a pious job. Probably, it never was. It is not expected to be fool-proof either. The views are not 'true and *correct*'. Instead, they are 'true and *fair*'. The 'correct picture' of audited accounts has given way to the 'fair picture'. Audit firms are business entities with revenue targets, providing opportunity for vertical movement to managers and partners on the basis of revenue they generate. Gopalakrishnan earned a huge sum for Price Waterhouse. Ethics are not for the high priests who formulate them for lesser mortals.

Although auditors, in general, are not corrupt, they could be susceptible to business pressures especially when they disagree with big clients at the levels of Chief Financial Officer (CFO) and Chief Executive Officer (CEO). The trouble starts then. Business issues surface and ethics are often compromised. The smaller the audit firm, the bigger is the client pressure on it. Large audit firms have large accounts and have on paper ability to stand up to manipulative clients. But it is not easy and also not in an audit firm's long term business interest to frequently take on more powerful and difficult CEOs or CFOs on accounting principles and practices. Big public image of clients and their top executives may also indirectly influence auditors in presenting a 'fair view' of financial statements.

There are so many public awards and accolades for corporate heads but no one has come forward to sponsor an award for the toughest of auditors or accounting purists. There are no special incentives for tough auditors from SEBI, ICAI, RBI and the Department of Corporate Affairs, Government of India. Therefore, it is no wonder that networking, financial engineering and innovative accounting is what clever audit partners are specialising in today. No one seems to do this better and more effectively than the Big Four. The acquisition or networking of smaller firms by the Big Four is constantly narrowing the scope for competition among public accounting firms. And, thanks to growing dependence on technology, organised accounting fraud is becoming more commonplace these days. The Sarbane-Oxley disclosure norms were initially considered too tough on US corporations but that did not dampen the innovative spirit of Bernard Madoff, the Ponzi scheme mastermind, or large US investment bankers, the losses of which brought the world economy under the knees. Madoff used accounting software to generate false computer statements on investment of funds for years until they were caught in their own trap in 2008. Did their auditors know about it?

The unholy relationship audit partners often enjoy with clients appears to be at the root of many missing or fictitious statements in the books of accounts of public corporations, banks and financial institutions. It tends to ignore the basic framework or premises for the preparation and presentation of financial statements which deals with (a) the objective, (b) qualitative characteristics determining the usefulness of information given in financial statements, (c) definition, recognition and measurements of the elements helping to construct such statements, and finally (d) concepts of capital and capital maintenance. The five fundamental principles of a professional accountant which concern integrity, objectivity, professional competence and due care, confidentiality and professional behaviour get automatically sacrificed when business compulsions or retention of mandates bear overriding influence on audit partners pushing ethical issues to the back seat.

ICAI may disagree, but accountants are no holy cows. They are part of the same society, the foundation for which is laid on political feuds, bribing MPs and MLAs to stay in power, unlimited greed and corruption. Even the so-called regulatory authorities are not free of rogues in their ranks, ever so ready to bend under external pressure and influence. If independent members on the board of a listed public enterprise are not truly independent, how can an audit partner be expected to be ruthlessly independent? Even a powerful market regulator such as SEBI could not have its way to implement its writ on appointment of independent directors on the board of listed companies in the face of resistance from large business houses and industry associations.

In the course of the investigation into the Satyam fraud, ICAI 'found' that the Big Four (MAFs) are merrily bending laws and providing auditing and other related services in India by tying up with local firms. The whole world knew about it. The government knew about it. The RBI knew about it. Industry knew about it. Why did it take so long for ICAI to note the development? Now that the 'mischief' has been detected, what penal action does ICAI contemplate against Indian audit associates of PwC, KPMG, E & Y and Deloitte? Could Price Waterhouse be barred from practising for one or two years? Or, was the Price-tag too strong for ICAI to challenge? More pertinently, what role has the government been playing to book the Big Four if they have been flouting laws to do business in India?

In so far as the government is concerned, there are two straight forward issues involved. First, are the Big Four truly circumventing their entry-level restrictions and bypassing laws to either conduct or influence corporate audit and accounting function, directly or indirectly? Secondly, are the Big Four indulging in such areas of consultancy which are not permitted under the existing laws? In such an event, the government can and should take legal and administrative action against the erring foreign audit firms which entered the country in the garb of consultants.

Why couldn't the Government of India act more like the US government after the Enron accounting fraud to frame appropriate accounting and disclosure laws for public corporations to protect millions of the country's ordinary investors from corporate fraud?

Why didn't the Government of India encourage highly competent persons in its ranks, comparable to US counterparts such as the former SEC chairman Arthur Levitt Jr, former US Federal Reserve chairman Paul Volcker, former Comptroller of the US David Walker, and Paul Sarbanes, former chairman of the US Congress committee on banking, housing and urban affairs, to review and rewrite the accounting and disclosure norms, construct a strong legal framework on the lines of the Sarbanes-Oxley Act and hand down exemplary punishment to law offenders? In the US, the administration, led by the President of America himself, asked the powerful Government Accounting Office (GAO) to look deeper into four major areas concerning corporate governance, independent audit of financial statements, oversight of the accounting profession and, finally, accounting and financial reporting issues, and advise the government on specific corrective measures.

Curiously, the Government of India showed no such initiative or interest to ensure reliability of public accounting practices. It could have at least asked the Comptroller and Auditor General of India to look into the country's biggest ever accounting fraud case involving a public company and advise the government on what could be done to prevent similar frauds in future. The government's Serious Frauds Office under the Ministry of Corporate Affairs did make an investigation, mostly on the basis of the CBI charge sheet, but its report was not made public. Even Indian Parliament, unlike the US Congress, did not ask the government to make a detailed statement on the Satyam accounting frauds case and demand action against the corporate management and its auditors.

CHAPTER V

India's Enron

Corporate accounting frauds all over the world follow a familiar pattern. They manipulate, misinterpret and misrepresent GAAP and established accounting standards in collusion with both internal and external auditors to cheat stockholders and stakeholders in order to benefit a few people in top management to amass illegal wealth. Colluding audit partners or audit firms naturally get a share of the booty. Large-scale corporate accounting frauds are practically impossible without the support and involvement of independent auditors.

There exist a lot of similarities between the role of Andersen in the Enron case and Price Waterhouse in the Satyam financial fraud. The modus operandi of the top management of both Enron and Satyam was generally similar. Both Price Waterhouse and Andersen played an active role in the business of their respective clients – Satyam Computers and Enron – through auditing and consulting. Both earned huge revenues from their respective clients on account of non-audit revenues. In 2000, Enron paid Andersen US$ 27 million for consulting services. The amount represented a little over 50 per cent of Andersen's revenue from this single client. Similarly, in 2007-08, Satyam Computers paid Price Waterhouse Rs 12.7 million for non-audit services, accounting for about 30 per cent of the audit firm's revenue from this single software technology client for that year.

The bankruptcy of Enron followed a systematic accounting fraud by the company's top management team, practised unabashedly and perpetrated over years, which Andersen failed to notice and report until it was too late. Andersen ignored the statements on accounting standards (SAS) of the US AICPA to allow the Enron bosses to carry on with the fraud. Kenneth Lay ran Enron like a dictator. Follow Lay's line or leave. That was the message to the top management team. Dynergy, a business rival, came to the rescue of Enron months before Enron filed the bankruptcy petition on 2 December 2001. It offered to bail them out with a US$ 10-billion buy-out deal. But, it was Kenneth Lay's confessionary public statement on 16 October that gave Enron no choice but to decrease shareholders' equity by US$ 1.2 billion to put a spanner in the works of the Dynergy take-over attempt. Finally, when Enron declared bankruptcy, it left a big hole of US$ 13.1 billion in debt on the company's books of accounts, US$ 18.1 billion on the books of accounts of its subsidiaries and some US$ 20 billion more off the balance sheets.

Enron's top management indulged in heavy insider trading and used the subsidiaries for the purpose. The balance sheet was artificially pumped up with inflated asset values. Liabilities were very cleverly transferred to subsidiaries without making a consolidation. It painted a false rosy picture of the company's financial health luring investors to invest more in the company's stocks and debt instruments. It was a masterpiece of financial engineering and book-cooking. The financial accounts of the subsidiaries, to which a large portion of liabilities were systematically transferred over the years, were given a miss in Enron's annual reports. Interestingly, a year later, Dynergy itself was facing a SEC investigation into accounting fraud executing 'round-trip' trades to artificially boost energy trading volume and cash flow. In 2002, Standard & Poor's (S&P) cut its credit rating to 'junk' grade. Dynergy said its cash flow was expected to fall by as much as US$ 400 million from the originally projected level of US$ 1 billion for the year.

Shareholders, creditors and regulatory authorities did not question the authenticity of Enron's balance sheets, audited and certified by Arthur

Andersen, then part of the global Big Five. Andersen partners, making fat revenues from the firm, played host to the mischief by the Enron top brass. The audit firm showed the middle finger to the American accounting safety valves – GAAP, GAAS and SAS – to violate the standard accounting protocol and stipulations by the American Institute of Certified Public Accountants (AICPA). Enron emerged as the second largest contributor to Andersen's annual revenue. Since rules are always subject to interpretations, Andersen was probably confident that it would be able to wriggle out of the sticky situation at the end. But that was borne more out of a false conviction than on material truth. Enron's end came faster than the audit firm had expected.

There were two possibilities before Andersen. One, the volatility of the situation could get substantially minimised if the Enron top brass could raise a few billion dollars from the market or from lending institutions. The second option, a sell-off deal with a big investor, looked more probable. Fortunately, for the world, none of the possibilities materialised to rescue Enron and its rogue auditors from their collapse.

Post-Enron, the governments, the investor community and the regulatory authorities across the world woke up to the bitter truth about the fragile capitalist system and the limitations of rules and statutes in the face of endless corporate greed and its perpetrators. This was to be repeated again seven years later after the big five US-based global investment banks collapsed one after another like a pack of cards because of sticky derivative deals. It would appear that the business and corporate world hardly learnt anything from the collapse of Enron and Xerox's falsification of financial results only a few years before.

Corporate balance sheets continued to appear more like corporate scandal sheets. The corporate world's journey through the 21st century with the promise of better and more reliable accounting practices, financial transparency and good governance received a serious jolt as one after another large companies in the US, which boasts the strictest of accounting standards and disclosure norms among industrialised nations, faced charges of accounting frauds. They included Xerox, Adelphia Communications, AOL Time Warner, Bristol-Myers Squibb,

Global Crossing, Halliburton, Kmart, Merck, Peregrine Systems, Tyco, Qwest Communications International, WorldCom and, of course, Enron and Arthur Andersen.

While Enron boosted profits, hid debts, engaged in off-the-book partnerships, manipulated energy markets in Texas and California and bribed foreign governments, allegedly including India, to win contracts, Arthur Andersen was convicted of obstruction of justice and ceased to be a public audit firm. The latter had illegally destroyed thousands of documents related to Enron audit after the SEC stepped in to launch an investigation. Enron investors and shareholders filed several lawsuits against Andersen, demanding millions of dollars in compensation.

Satyam Computers' Ramalinga Raju initiated bookkeeping fraud in 2000-01, around the same time when Kenneth Lay brought down Enron. Raju too ran his enterprise like a dictator. Follow him or exit. All of Raju's direct reporting officers took the message seriously. Almost all the Satyam Computers board members, whole-time or independent, and senior executives came or originated from the same Indian state, Andhra Pradesh, Raju's state of origin, and spoke the same language. Even the audit partners were no exception. Company insiders, on condition of anonymity, allege the audit partners were 'hand-picked' by Raju. Everyone at Satyam feared Raju. No one opened his mouth until Raju opened his own to confess the lies in Satyam's books of accounts.

In the case of Enron, Andersen belatedly questioned the book entries in 2000. And, its CFO refused to fall in line with the CEO. Both were too late. These are some of the few major dissimilar acts that could be noticed by those trying to list the similarities in the two corporate accounting fraud stories that took place in two different times, at two different places, under two different systems of management and also under two different regulatory systems. Other fraudulent practices and acts followed a similar pattern. Both Andersen and Price Waterhouse were highly reliable brands in the public financial audit business until the collapse of Enron and Satyam.

As in Enron, Satyam Computers' income was inflated, liabilities were understated, the cash book was inflated, stock prices were artificially held high, insider trading by Satyam top guns was rampant, corporate fund was siphoned out by promoters to create personal assets and an aborted merger proposal made to prevent the collapse of the Indian multinational computer software services enterprise, all with the support, direct or indirect, of the company's independent auditors. For Enron, Dynergy failed to play the role of a White Knight because of Kenneth Lay's confession. In the case of Satyam Computers, Ramalinga Raju had to make the bizarre accounting fraud confession as the Maytas companies' attempt to play a White Knight to save Satyam failed to materialise.

If Price Waterhouse in India did not meet the same fate as Andersen in the US, it is because of India's weak regulatory system and general apathy. India's SEBI is not the USA's SEC. In India, the audit firm could even get away with openly challenging SEBI's jurisdiction to investigate and take disciplinary action against the firm. Like Price Waterhouse in India, Andersen doggedly fought against the regulatory authorities to prove its innocence until a jury verdict convicted the audit firm. Its defence lawyer insisted that the firm "did not commit a crime". Large investors in Satyam Computers, who could afford the cost of lawsuits, did not show the alacrity to sue Price Waterhouse, demanding millions of rupees in compensation for the audit firm's alleged role in the Satyam accounting fraud. It may be because of the quick action by the Indian government in organising a sell-off and getting a high profile investor such as Tech Mahindra to rescue Satyam, providing substantial relief to the latter's employees and shareholders.

Scam-stars in India are too thick-skinned to succumb to the pressure of public criticism. And if they have strong political connections, as they do have in most cases including Satyam, they can get away with blue murder. India's telecommunications minister A Raja had hung on to power with his political party's support for years despite his alleged involvement in a multi-billion dollar spectrum allotment scam. The Comptroller & Auditor General of India (CAG), the country's super government auditor, estimated a loss of up to US$ 39 billion to the exchequer due to alleged indiscretion showed in allotment of spectrum to certain private parties, including overseas bidders. These private telecom companies paid only around US$ 350 million to the government for pan-India operating licences in 2008. Some of the licence holders then resold their licences or brought in foreign investors to make billions of dollars. A special audit by the CAG estimated a loss of about US$ 39 billion to the exchequer by way of procedural manipulation and under-pricing of these licences. In a way, it is also another India's Enron. It seems India is fast catching up with the USA in corporate scams. And the role of audit firms in corporate financial frauds in both the countries is suspect.

In India, large audit firms are, however, more defiant to the regulatory system than their counterparts in the US. Price Waterhouse did not think twice before taking SEBI to Bombay High Court, challenging the market regulator's power to inquire and act against the audit firm as all such matters could only be adjudicated by the Institute of Chartered Accountants of India (ICAI). While upholding the powers of SEBI to institute an enquiry against the audit firm, a High Court division Bench, which heard the case, asked SEBI not to commence its proceedings against Price Waterhouse for four weeks to give a chance to the audit firm to file an appeal, if it wanted, against the order in the Supreme Court of India. SEBI had earlier issued show cause notices to the audit firm as to why action should not be taken up against Price Waterhouse for violation of SEBI regulations (Prohibition of Fraudulent and Unfair Trade Practices Relating to Securities Market). The audit firm was charged with 'gross negligence' and 'misconduct' for facilitating 'the management of Satyam to create an artificial demand in the scrip of Satyam and to create false and misleading price discovery with regard to its scrip'.

The SEBI charges were almost similar to those the SEC had levelled against Enron. SEBI had accused Price Waterhouse of 'failing to independently verify the bank statements, fixed deposits, debtors' position and invoices of Satyam which led to the false picture being presented (about the company's financial health)'. If found guilty, SEBI could prohibit the audit firm from issuing certificates to listed companies for a specific period and also restrain it from dealing in securities.

Price Waterhouse did not relent. It said only ICAI, the self regulatory body, had the power to conduct any such investigation. The most interesting part of its submission was that Satyam Computers' audit was carried out by another Price Waterhouse firm, located in Bangalore with a different registration number. And, as such, other Price Waterhouse partnership firms could not be held responsible for the alleged failings of the Bangalore firm. Does it not make a mockery of the christening of an audit firm, sub-letting its precious name or brand to independent partners with independent registrations following independent business practices? The principal owner of a brand or a corporate name must be liable for the protection of the value attached to the name by clients, associates and society at large. Brand or name protection is ultimately expected to be the function of its owners and not its franchisees or lessees. Price Waterhouse is a big brand in the financial audit and accounting industry, reflecting its operational integrity and high standards, for which corporate and other clients pay large fees to audit partners. This is not to be confused with technicalities such as its registration number and location of registration. The global body, PwC, would know better. Or, ICAI may be better placed to respond to the Price Waterhouse claim before the Bombay High Court. Does PwC follow the same business practice in the USA as its associate (or associates) in India?

Many in India wonder whether the fall of mighty Enron and IT major Satyam could have been prevented if their respective audit firms, Andersen and Price Waterhouse, did their job more diligently and their audit reports served an early warning to shareholders, creditors, management, employees and the regulatory authorities. Although Andersen paid a heavy price for its malpractice in not presenting the fair view of the accounts of Enron, Price Waterhouse in India, on the contrary, even refuses to share the burden of passing the falsified accounts of Satyam year after year leading to its collapse.

Incidentally, Price Waterhouse is a registered practicing chartered accountancy firm in India unlike other well-known foreign names such as Ernst & Young and KPMG, which operate through member firms such as S R Batliboi & Co and BSR & Co. ICAI had recently questioned the modus operandi of those foreign accounting firms doing business in the country without registration 'through surrogate means'. ICAI president Amarjit Chopra had openly repudiated the business practices of the other Big Three – KPMG, E&Y and Deloitte. Chopra recommended action against those unregistered foreign accountancy firms and told the government that they should be barred from doing business in India. The ICAI president said while local member firms sign audit reports, the assignments are usually taken on behalf of their respective foreign associates or mentors. As a result, no action for auditing lapses and oversights can be taken against the overseas parents who are not registered with ICAI and do not take up business directly.

Non ICAI-registered foreign audit firms disagree. Having a member firm in India is not illegal. Those non-registered firms do only consultancy jobs and not auditing function directly. The question is, are they responsible for the lapses of their respective member audit firms? The case of Price Waterhouse, which is registered with ICAI, appears to be even more complicated after its submission before the Bombay High Court. The issue raised there was which Price Waterhouse?

CHAPTER VI

Fairly Untrue

Knowledge of accounting and auditing, as in the case of any other discipline, is continuously evolving. The complex nature of modern business practices, including attaching correct value to derivatives, futures and options, intangibles, risks and uncertainties, does not make accounting practice any easier. There is always a controversy between 'fair value' and 'market value' as also between 'fair reporting' and 'correct reporting'.

In India, where the laws governing companies substantially owe their existence to the practices followed under British colonial rule, the 'fair value' attached to an asset is hardly fair. The value appreciation of land and buildings, for the purpose of computing income tax relief at the time of their sale or transfer, represents only a fraction of their true value at current market price. The valuation of reputation or brand is always a complex process. Also, it is not always psychologically convincing. Imagine Coca-Cola's brand value being bigger than Microsoft's! An accountant-cum-valuer would know better. What he wants the public to take as 'true and fair' may neither be all that true nor that fair either.

Business compulsions and complexities are bound to influence in-house accountants and force them to invent or apply innovative practices, making the task of professional public accountants even more difficult. Disclosures rarely represent the whole truth. Maybe, they are not expected to either. Since laws are subject to interpretations and circumventions, it would be too much to expect any permanent legal remedy to accounting malpractices or auditing oversights, deliberate or otherwise. The disclosures required under the tough Sarbanes-Oxley Act in the US could not do away with corporate financial jugglery altogether.

Controversies are already brewing in the United States over the jurisdiction and effectiveness of the Dodd-Frank Wall Street Reform and Consumer Protection Act – in short, the Dodd-Frank Act – signed into law on 21 July 2010. If Basel II, the second of the Basel Committee accords on banking supervision and recommendation of banking laws and regulations, failed to prevent the recent collapse of some of the global banks on both sides of the Atlantic, there is no guarantee that Dodd-Frank or Basel III, which also came into effect in July 2010, will be able to discipline the bonus-hungry bankers and their accomplices among the public accounting community to stop recurrence of another banking scandal of a national or international scale.

In December 2009, the Basel Committee on Banking Supervision approved a slew of proposals to further strengthen global capital and liquidity regulations towards making the banking sector more resilient to the crisis related to regulation, supervision and risk management of global banks. The idea was to improve the quality, consistency and transparency of the capital base. The committee proposed to strengthen the capital requirements for counterparty credit risk exposures from derivatives, repos (repurchase options exercised by a country's central bank) and securities financing activities. It also proposed to introduce a number of measures, including a new leverage ratio to contain the build-up of excessive leverage in the banking system, additional safeguards against risk and measurement error, the creation of capital buffers in good times that may be useful at times of stress and a countercyclical capital framework to contribute to a more stable banking system.

The governors and heads of supervision, the oversight body of the Basel Committee, the Financial Stability Board and G-20 leaders were still not happy with the reform process. They did not want to lag behind what Dodd-Frank was contemplating to do in the USA. The net result was Basel III, an amended version of the reform package proposed in December 2009. It called for an 'unweighted' leverage ratio; two new capital buffers; new and substantial capital charges for non-cleared derivative and other financial market transactions; and significant revisions of the rules on the types of instrument that count as bank capital.

All these are welcome safeguards against another collapse of the financial system. But, they miss out on one vital aspect – integrity. No law can guarantee integrity of professional bookkeepers, top financial accountants and auditors. The problem is not that of the inadequacy of laws, rules, regulations and guidelines. The problem is far deeper and extremely complex. It relates to personal greed and professional integrity.

Simply put, banking is all about balancing assets with liabilities. For instance, deposits with banks are a liability. On the contrary, bank credit to customers is an asset. Bank's equity capital and investments are also assets. Credit is generally given against mortgages. The latter could be undervalued or overvalued. The same applies with the valuation of investments. Bank credits mostly carry a risk element. Any bank management, in connivance with financial accountants and auditors, can manipulate these valuations, underreport risks, overstate income and show sticky loans as good loans at least for the time being.

Derivatives, as the legendary Warren Buffet of Berkshire Hathaway had once put it, are like 'financial weapons of mass destruction'. The serial global investment bank failure of 2008 leading to the collapse of a part of the world financial system and economic slow-down showed how prophetic was Buffet in his remark. Banks were into gambling despite Basel I and Basel II. And, all the while their financial accountants and auditors kept looking the other way.

The 2,000-page Dodd-Frank Act provides a framework to safeguard the financial system and prevent a 2008-like collapse of some of the giant Wall Street banks. The creation of a systemic risk supervisor called the Financial Stability Oversight Council is one of the major highlights of the Act, which is expected to give birth of some 250 rules and regulations. The question is: to what extent will the Dodd-Frank Act be able to truly mould mischievous minds of bank management, its top accountants and its auditors to ensure stronger mandates for transparency and oversight in derivatives and hedge funds markets? Can the Act govern individual integrity or conscience of a banker and external auditor?

The 2010 year-end reports in the *Wall Street Journal* (WSJ) and *New York Times* (NYT) brought out the most disturbing story about the real culprits behind the collapse of the giant Wall Street Investment Bank, Lehman Brothers. It seems that the regulators were more peeved about the role played by the audit firm, Ernst & Young, in Lehman's sad demise than the false and misleading statements provided by the bank's senior executives. E & Y, Lehman's external auditor, certified the bank's financial statements from 2001 until it filed the bankruptcy petition with the US Bankruptcy Court in Manhattan on 15 September 2008. The role of the audit firm was under severe scrutiny since the release in March 2010 of a 2,200-page investigation report into the affairs of the bank leading to its collapse. The Securities and Exchange Commission and the Justice Department were involved in the investigation into the failure of Lehman Brothers. The NYT report said that the government investigations into Lehman 'resulted in no charges against any of the firm's executives, including Richard S Fuld Jr, its long time chief executive'.

While the investigation report accused the bank's top-level executives and financial officers of doctoring the global financial institution's balance sheet and inflating the value of Lehman's souring real-estate holdings, among other alleged misdeeds, it came down heavily on E & Y for its failure to take cognisance of them. The report specifically focused on certain materially misleading accounting manoeuvre which temporarily removed assets worth US$ 50 billion from the balance sheet to give an impression that Lehman had reduced its debt levels. Appropriately though, it did not escape the careful eyes of the bankruptcy court-appointed examiner who found that Lehman Brothers often indulged in such practices just before the end of a financial quarter every year to mislead investors and stakeholders. And, E & Y did not take any step 'to question or challenge the non-disclosure by Lehman of its use of US$ 50 billion of temporary, off-balance sheet transactions'.

The NYT news story said that at the time of the release of the examiner's report, "the Ernst & Young spokesman said that the firm stood by its work and complied with generally accepted accounting principles". He also said that Lehman's collapse was the result of "a series of unprecedented adverse events in the financial markets". Not many were impressed leave alone being convinced by E & Y's standard 'holding statement' as dutifully dished out by the firm's spokesman. The New York Attorney General's office was certainly not. At the time of going to the press, the Attorney General's office was contemplating to file a civil liability suit against the audit firm.

When a global firm indulges in accounts manipulation, it does so at a global scale. If Enron's financial jugglery did not spare its investment in its erstwhile Indian subsidiary, Dhabol Power Company in Maharashtra, an independent US Securities and Exchange Commission investigation into some of the transactions of Lehman Brothers found an India connection with regard to overvaluation of its investment in an Indian power company, which might have also contributed to the US firm's artificially bolstered finances before its collapse in 2008. Lehman, then the fourth largest US investment bank with over 25,000 employees worldwide, did invest in energy sector projects in several emerging economies, including China and India, as did other US biggies such as Goldman Sachs, JP Morgan Chase, Morgan Stanley, Citigroup and Bank of America.

Lehman Brothers had a combined equity stake of 18.9 per cent in the Hyderabad-based KSK Energy Ventures Limited through two of its subsidiaries. The bigger of the two subsidiaries was based at the Indian Ocean Island, Mauritius, a tax haven, the largest router of overseas funds in India's both primary and secondary markets. This subsidiary was known as LB Mauritius III Limited. When Lehman invested in KSK Energy Venture, the Indian company was implementing a twin-location power generation programme – one at Chhattisgarh and the other at Jharkhand – having a combined capacity of 1,250 MW. Unconfirmed reports suggest that Lehman invested or committed funds in two tranches totalling between US$ 75 million and US$ 93 million in KSK Energy.

If Lehman had truly overvalued its investment in an Indian power project, it was most unlikely without the knowledge, consent and even participation of the majority Indian promoter of the project. An overvaluation of existing shares by a company tapping the equity market for further capital infusion for project implementation or capacity expansion is not an uncommon practice in India. It is generally done by inflating present financial performance and future projections, which rarely meet the so-called targets. New investors go by the project assessment by merchant banks and market price of shares. Overvaluation of its investment in an Indian power company was likely to have benefitted both Lehman and the other equity partners in the project. It could not have been done without a well-crafted window dressing of financial statements at both ends, involving key accounting professionals, including auditors. Not many investors in India may be aware of the SEC's strong suspicion of Lehman's hefty asset value inflation in an Indian power project.

The Financial Reporting Council of the United Kingdom, the country's independent accounting regulator, is also said to be investigating into E & Y's role in preparing reports about Lehman's European operations for the British regulators. It will come as a big image jolt before the entire assembly of public accounting firms world over if E & Y gets involved in lawsuits without a settlement. E & Y will most certainly not meet the fate of Arthur Andersen on the issue of its alleged professional misconduct leading to the bankruptcy of the once mighty Lehman Brothers, although the New York Attorney General's office may not lose sleep if the improbable happens. Even Arthur Andersen's conviction on the obstruction of justice charges failed to stand the ultimate judicial scrutiny. The lower court's verdict was thrown out by the US Supreme Court although the audit firm's fate was sealed by then.

It was the New York Attorney General, Andrew M Cuomo, who reportedly contemplated filing a civil fraud lawsuit against E & Y before he became New York's Governor. Cuomo's uncompromising stance against high earning, often unethical, Wall Street money managers has endeared him to millions of ordinary investors whose lives revolve around stock indices and the economic trends they reflect. In the past, Cuomo had sued the Bank of America and its former chief executive Kenneth D Lewis, accusing them of hiding billions of dollars in losses of Merrill Lynch from shareholders without regard to SEC's prior settlement with the investment bank. Frankly, the general public would support any regulatory or judicial action against those greedy money managers and rogue public accounting firms who misuse their trust and play foul with their hard earned savings and investments.

The news of E & Y's alleged involvement in Lehman's manipulated financial statement has sent shockwaves all over the world. Many thought the public audit and accounting firms would be more careful in performing their statutory task after the collapse of Arthur Andersen. But money managers and public accounting professionals do not seem to learn. They continue to provide advice to wrong-doing clients and certify their balance sheets and financial statements as 'true and fair'. They go with the corporate management and its finance team to earn fat fees at the cost of their fiduciary integrity and responsibility to ordinary shareholders. Whenever in trouble, they take shelter under the stock statement that they went by 'generally accepted accounting principles' (GAAP) and stood by their work. The code of professional ethics is more often sacrificed at the altar of greed.

Whatever be E & Y's role in Lehman Brothers' going bankrupt, the 158-year-old financial institution succumbed to the subprime mortgage crisis in September 2008. It was the biggest bankruptcy filing in history. The pre-bankruptcy assets of Lehman Brothers Holding Inc were worth over US$ 639 billion. Initially, Barclays Plc and Bank of America showed some interest in taking over Lehman but later abandoned the idea.

That year also saw the collapse of Washington Mutual (WaMu), which listed over $327 billion in assets in its bankruptcy filing. The next to fall was Thornburg Mortgage that went bankrupt in April 2009 with US$ 36.5 billion in assets and the lender CIT Group which went bankrupt in November 2009, listing US$ 71 billion in assets. Did the annual financial statements of these firms certified by their respective external auditors provide a 'true and fair' view of the state of affairs of these firms?

Increasing dependence of audit firms and of their partners on total fees from a client, close business relationship with a client, potential employment of family members and friends with a client and fear about losing a client, especially if the assurance client is large and has unassailable corporate reputation, can influence the professional behaviour and judgement of public accounting practitioners.

There are self-review threats as well. They could come from detection of 'error' in the course of revaluation of a public accountant's work, detection of fault in financial systems after being involved in their design and implementation, or providing a service for a client which directly affects the subject matter of the assurance engagement and accepting gifts or preferential treatment from a client. There could also be intimidation threat, including legal action, against a key member or members of an audit team.

It is not that there are no safeguards against such threats to the integrity of public accounting professionals. Regulatory authorities all over the world are concerned about the growing threats to professionals engaged in public accounting practice. However, the safeguards will have to come from the leaders of the public accounting firms themselves. They do exist on paper through documented policies and procedures with all public accounting firms. The key message is that public accountants will 'work in the public interest' and comply with the fundamental principles of accounting.

The leadership of an audit and accounting firm have documented policies with regard to identification of threats to compliance of fundamental principles, valuation of the significance of threats, monitoring of threats and prescription of safeguards, including legal protection. The leadership of a public accounting firm is expected to stand by and protect its accounting professionals working on assignment against unethical suggestions from manipulative clients. But these threat and safeguard perceptions seem to lose relevance when a single client of an audit firm in one location accounts for as much as 10 per cent or even more of its annual revenue from the same location.

The 21st Century, with all its emphasis on and promises of better governance and transparency in financial transactions, corporate ethics and corporate social responsibility, has in its very first decade witnessed an amazingly high record of corporate financial frauds and accounting failure where bookkeeping appeared to be all about bookcooking. The list of such corporate entities and financial institutions is pretty long. The most prominent among them are Lehman Brothers Holdings Inc, Enron, Bernie Madoff, Satyam Computers, Worldcom, Barlow Clowes, Daewoo to some extent, Fannie Mae & Freddie Mac and AIG. However, few individuals responsible for the financial fraud and the leadership of the audit firms who failed to detect such large-scale misstatement of accounts received exemplary punishment, barring possibly Bernie Madoff who was sentenced to 150 years in prison. A typical cynical view of the reason behind the harsh sentence against Madoff was that it was because he had mostly robbed powerful American millionaires and billionaires and not the less fortunate common man.

The Worldcom accounting fraud covered some US$ 11 billion in false profits and margins. The company's balance sheets and annual reports were masked by giving a totally wrong picture of its financial health. The cases of the two financial services firms, Fannie Mae and Freddic Mac, were even more interesting. The two firms held over a half of the USA's US$ 12 trillion mortgages before their collapse in 2008. The firms had to be placed in conservatorship by the US Federal Housing Finance Agency. It may be said that they were taken over by the federal government.

Peter Clowes, co-owner of UK's Barlow Clowes, had allegedly spent some US$100 million of his clients' money in items such as luxury yachts, private aircraft and cars which ultimately led to the collapse of the company. The South Korean Chaebol and its second largest industrial conglomerate, Daewoo, collapsed and got dismantled towards the end of 1999 due to its inability to handle the worldwide financial crisis and labour unrest. The downgrading of its 'credit rating' to 'AA (-)' led to the drying-up of funds of one of America's top financial institutions, insurance giant AIG, and its ultimate collapse after the disclosure of its huge financial losses and frauds in 2008. AIG was once the world's 18th largest corporation.

Corporate financial frauds affect employees and ordinary shareholders the most. Over 15,000 of Enron employees, who had most of their savings in company stocks, almost turned paupers overnight as the power company's share price fell from US$ 83 in early 2001 to US$ 0.01 in October 2001. When the owners of Phar-Mor, one of America's largest pharmacy chains boasting over 300 drug stores in the early 1990s, were accused of large-scale financial embezzlement, deceptive inventories and fudged data leading to the firm's collapse, over 25,000 employees were affected.

In India, millions lost jobs in the 1970s and 1980s when a few hundred old family-managed enterprises in the fields of engineering, steel, mining, jute and cotton textiles, tea plantation, shipping and financial services were practically abandoned as unviable by their erstwhile owners leaving massive holes in the pockets of commercial banks in the form of non-performing assets. This forced the government to take over nearly 250 financially sick corporations and nationalise dozens of private banks mainly to protect jobs and savings of small depositors.

Not a single employer suffered. On the contrary, they were extremely relieved. No one went to jail for the systematic loot of public funds, including large bank credits, by their owner-managers. The series of take-over of sick industrial enterprises had, in fact, helped these entrepreneur-managers easily shake off the liabilities from their shoulders on to the government lap. And, thereafter, they became free and even richer with 'stolen' corporate assets to diversify into newer and faster profit-making businesses.

Times have changed, but not management practices. The promoter-managers of one of India's largest joint stock metal companies, Ispat Industries, with a nameplate steelmaking capacity of 3.3 million tons per annum, walked out of the company towards the end of 2010 leaving a combined Rs 7,000-crores (nearly US$ 1.8 billion) hole into the pockets of its bankers and creditors. The temporarily closed steel company was rescued by a rival group firm, JSW Steel, making the company's helpless looking lenders to work out on debt restructuring with the new owners.

The government of India suspected large-scale funds embezzlement by the steel company's original promoters allegedly in connivance with banks and their subsequent illegal transfer to overseas destinations as the taxmen conducted simultaneous raids in the premises maintained by the company and its owners in various locations of the country. The tax raids were reported in the Times of India. If the government's suspicions prove correct, the balance sheets and annual financial statements certified by the company's external auditors presented anything but a true and fair picture of the state of affairs of the enterprise and its alleged 'missing' funds. The same may be said about the account books of Ispat Industries' bankers.

Generally, banks are involved in most large scale corporate financial fraud cases. Despite the existence of a plethora of regulatory controls, banks and financial institutions are becoming increasingly irresponsible in handling public funds either by their clients or by themselves. A somewhat Ponzi-style Rs. 400 crore (nearly $90 million) financial fraud involving a single Citibank branch at Gurgaon, bordering Delhi, was allowed to be accumulated over a period of time until it was unearthed during the Christmas of 2010. The Citibank fraud attracted wide media coverage in India. The news shook up the whole corporate world and many high networth individuals (HNI) as they were allegedly 'duped' into a bogus deposit scheme by the bank offering very high returns.

In another case, an angry investor, Sanjeev Aggarwal, a HNI and co-founder of venture capital fund Helion Venture Partners, lodged a criminal complaint with the Gurgaon police against Citibank top brass, including the American bank's global CEO Vikram Pandit, chairman William Rhodes, chief operating officer Douglas Peterson, chief financial officer John Gerspach and CEO India Pramit Jhaveri, for 'cheating' as much as Rs. 32 crore (over $7 million) of his personal money. Aggarwal, in his complaint, said Citibank used his investment to buy securities which were never transferred to him. The money was allegedly taken out of Aggarwal's wealth management account with the US bank. The venture capitalist was the founder and CEO of Daksh, a firm that was acquired by IBM sometime ago.

The growing corporate financial scandals and accounting frauds in India prompted the country's Finance Minister Pranab Mukherjee to use an ICAI platform to caution accounting firms against 'window dressing' of accounts and ask them to strictly follow disclosure guidelines. It was ICAI's first conference in 2011. The topic chosen for the conference was about sustained economic growth. Corporate Affairs Minister Salman Khurshid and Secretary to the Corporate Affairs Department D Bandyopadhya were among the top official participants. But, the Finance Minister seemed to attach equal importance, if not more, to good corporate governance as to the need for achieving a sustained double-digit economic growth.

Mukherjee said "accountants have a critical role in guarding against window dressing of balance sheets that encourage entities to take more and more risk until they are dangerously leveraged." The finance minister called for stronger disclosure standards for sophisticated financial products and transparent money trail but accepted the fact that "government and regulators can lay rules and frameworks, but can't mandate integrity and ethical conduct."

One can only wish that law could govern integrity, personal probity and human conscience.

Postscript

When a third generation entrepreneur from eastern India, aiming to set up a US$ 1.3-billion integrated steel plant in the region, was recently offered a US$ 50-million investment proposal by a foreign financial institution (FII); he and his team of senior executives appeared to be happy. Two FII representatives, who came to visit the entrepreneur, were accorded a warm private welcome. However, their otherwise fruitful official level discussion ended in a sour note as the FII men insisted that the company must give the audit mandate of the new steel company to a foreign firm, any of the Big Four. The promoters, who run one of the country's best performing joint stock engineering companies, had no intention to surrender their right to appoint the auditors to foreign investors for US$ 50 million. "Appointment of auditors is our business and certainly not of small outside investors. We have full faith in our auditors. If they don't have, it is their problem", said the chief executive of the company. The deal was off.

Foreign investors are generally more comfortable with foreign audit firms and their associates. Why is it so? What is the catch? Why is this auditor-client alliance necessary? How does it work? Is such an alliance good for corporate governance?

Eminent audit and accounting professional Samir Ganguly feels there is nothing wrong in an 'auditor-client alliance' as long as it does not compromise on 'professional and ethical standards of the audit function'. Such an alliance should not lead to an unholy nexus between the two. Ganguly, former joint managing partner of Ray & Ray, an associate of British financial audit and accounting firm Moore Stephen, says that client-auditor alliance is nothing new: "It was there. It is there. And, it is going to be there, no matter how many rules and laws are framed to break the alliance. The fact is clients need auditors. It is a statutory requirement. Audit firms need clients. They are in business which is always highly competitive. The existence of a nexus, though undesirable, is not uncommon under the present system."

The auditor community does not deny that companies sometimes window-dress their accounts with auditors' support to achieve certain short-term goals. In order to get larger accommodation from banks, a company may inflate sales income, profitability, get certain expenses capitalised and convert government grants or refundable items into income. There are other examples. Practicing auditors, on the other hand, have business objectives too. As in any other profession, there are dishonest persons in the auditing function as well. In large companies, the arm twisting starts from the internal audit function.

The smaller an audit firm, more are the chances of its getting manipulated by clients. Competition among such audit firms is very strong. Fees are small. Work is complex and heavy. Lately, many such firms have diversified into non-audit functions to sustain their operations. Many clients take advantage of this situation. Moreover, technology has changed the very profile of the business. Large audit firms have as many chartered accountants as software experts and data processors. To retain them, audit firms are forced to fork out large sums of money towards payment of salaries and perks. The employee cost forms a big component of expenditure of audit firms. The 'other income' becomes extremely important for the survival and growth of audit firms. Many large clients prefer appointment of multiple auditors. Smaller firms naturally lose out in the competition. Many are forced to be satisfied with internal audit assignments.

Alliance with auditors has become fundamental to the growth and market perception of many corporations. Former ICAI president Ved Jain says that thanks to technology and high level of expertise, audit function is capable of detecting any financial fraud or malpractice by a client. In this context, the accounts books of Satyam Computers as passed by its auditors have exposed the myth about the honesty and integrity of the Big Four and other multinational audit firms and their local associates, Jain points out. New Delhi-based Jain is in agreement with many senior professionals in the trade that rotation of auditors after three to five years could act as a deterrent to a possible client-auditor nexus. He likens the conspiracy between auditors and clients with criminal intent and says such conspirators should be booked under the appropriate provisions of the Indian Penal Code and punished. He denied the perception that the ICAI has been soft on big firms.

The CAG is, however, more forthright on the issue of a wide-spread nexus between clients and auditors and said it is more common in the private sector than in the public sector. There may be rare cases of such alliance between auditors and public sector management, but they do not go undetected, says Vinod Rai, the Comptroller & Auditor General of India. He is of the view that the auditor-client nexus in the private sector, if and wherever it exists, is the product of the selection and retention process of auditors. "If the industry and the government want, the CAG can help in the selection of auditors. Our selection process is most transparent and impartial. We are prepared to work with corporate management, auditors, regulatory bodies such as SEBI, ICAI and the department of corporate affairs to ensure compliance of best accounting standard and practice, help improve corporate accountability and ensure better governance", offers the country's super auditor. The CAG is of the view that no corporate accounting malpractice, hidden fund transfers, questionable contracts, suspicious deals and assets valuation in cases of M&A, under invoicing and over invoicing and receiving kick-backs at home and abroad, can escape the trained eyes of auditors if they discharge their duties diligently.

To improve the reliability of audited corporate accounts and balance sheets, the CAG strongly recommends not only periodical rotation of auditors, but also periodical special audits and peer reviews. Supplementary audit is very important. There should be a 'firewall' built in the system to minimise the scope for manipulation by clients. Audit committee at corporate board level has a very important role to play in the system. It is difficult to hoodwink at every checkpoint in the system. The CAG is also of the view that the arbitrary power to recruit and appoint auditors must be taken away from corporate board of directors to "break the umbilical cord". Joint-stock companies can choose auditors from the CAG's panel, if they so wish, seek help from SEBI and the department of corporate affairs, if necessary. In the financial sector, timely detection of sticky assets and its correct and up to date reporting can prevent sudden collapse of banks and financial institutions. The Reserve Bank of India (RBI), the country's central bank, is doing good work in keeping a close tab on financial accounts of banks, including co-operative banks.

Not all of CAG's radical prescriptions are palatable to industry, corporations as well as auditors' fraternity. However, a reform of the current bookkeeping, accounting and audit system is imminent. The proposed Companies Act, in supersession of the 55-year-old Companies Act, is expected to treat the issue seriously and incorporate several provisions to ensure greater transparency in the corporate financial reporting system and stakeholders' confidence in audit reports. Interestingly, the proposed Act has taken a less serious attitude towards the compliance of the corporate governance code, which has not been made mandatory, by leaving it for the time being to the good sense of a desirably socially responsible community of business leaders.

To what extent the government initiated corporate reform will achieve its objective is a billion-dollar question. The time-tested government-business-auditor alliance is too strong to be dismantled by a bunch of rules and regulations alone. The bookkeeping scandal at Satyam Computers showed how ineffective these rules and regulations are in the wilful absence of their compliance. The income tax department, the provident fund authorities, the registrar of companies, Satyam's bankers, credit rating agencies and stock exchanges all accepted the company's audited accounts on their face value for years.

The CAG itself has received little commendation from the government for the excellent job that it has been silently performing year after year, relentlessly exposing financial irregularities in government and public sector accounts with hardly any big impact on the concerned departmental bosses and the corporate management. Routinely, CAG reports form the basis of investigation into government accounts by the Public Accounts Committee (PAC) of Parliament. Since PAC is headed by an Opposition leader in Parliament, its critical reports rarely get the attention of the government or the ruling political power that it deserves. These reports are mostly preserved to decorate the Parliament library and to gather dust as time passes by.

Satyam's accounting fraud story is not the first of its kind. Nor does it promise to be the last. Many of the perpetrators of the Satyam Computers financial fraud and their conduits are still at large. Those few arrested nearly two years ago are yet to be convicted till the time of this book going to the press. No IT company, no apex industry organisation, no responsible member or members of the audit fraternity, especially the Big Four, has condemned the act.

Financial corruption is too common to be condemned by the industry. It is often practised openly and shamelessly by big business houses. It is probably only in India that one will see private entrepreneurs in the power utility sector, which are specially favoured by the government with guaranteed return on investment through a tariff fixation formula, misuse the corporate fund with impunity by diversifying into unrelated areas such as groceries, retail, real estate development and grab surplus land acquired at concessional rates from the government for other commercial use. And, all this happens with the full cooperation of the government and auditors. The common man is made to bear the cost of financial malpractice. Why should such entrepreneurs be critical about others?

Corporate governance will remain a far cry in our society until corporate conscience controls corporate greed.

Annexures

I. CASH & BANK BALANCE IN BALANCE SHEET*

Year	Cash balance in current Accounts as shown in the Balance Sheet (Rs in Crore) (a)	Cash available in FDR's as shown in the Balance Sheet (Rs in Crore) (b)	Cash and Bank Balance as shown in the Balance Sheet (Rs in Crore) (a+b)
2000-2001	140.82	0.73	141.55
2001-2002	250.63	820.55	1071.18
2002-2003	230.84	1262.61	1493.45
2003-2004	313.74	1469.16	1782.90
2004-2005	397.68	1804.38	2202.07
2005-2006	1021.28	1907.42	2928.70
2006-2007	415.18	3365.82	3781.00
2007-2008	956.29	3317.70	4273.99
Q1-2008	1338.62	3318.77	4657.39
Q2-2008	1841.17	3319.17	5160.34

* Source: Central Bureau of Investigation.
Chargesheet in RC-04(S) 2009, CBI/MDIT-Hyderabad

II. ACTUAL BALANCE

Year	Actual Cash Balances in Current Accounts (Rs in Crore) (a)	Actual Cash available in FDRs (Rs in Crore) (b)	Actual Cash and Bank Balances (Rs in Crore) (a+b)
2000-2001	27.04	0.67	27.71
2001-2002	34.47	38.59	73.06
2002-2003	63.87	25.93	89.80
2003-2004	49.50	22.71	72.22
2004-2005	75.91	11.91	87.82
2005-2006	69.32	111.92	181.24
2006-2007	172.13	57.45	229.57
2007-2008	127.39	9.36	136.75
Q1-2008	108.39	10.40	118.79
Q2-2008	128.96	10.82	139.78

III OVERSTATED CASH & BANK BALANCE

Year	Cash and Bank Balance shown in Balance Sheet (Rs in Crore) (a)	Actual Cash and Bank balances (Rs. in Crore) (b)	Difference (Rs. Crore) (a-b)
2000-2001	141.55	27.71	113.84
2001-2002	1071.18	73.06	998.12
2002-2003	1493.44	89.80	1403.64
2003-2004	1782.90	72.22	1710.68
2004-2005	2202.07	87.82	2214.24
2005-2006	2928.70	181.24	2747.46
2006-2007	3781.00	229.57	3551.43
2007-2008	4273.99	136.75	4137.23
Q1-2008	4657.39	118.79	4538.60
Q2-2008	5160.34	139.78	5020.55

IV FALSE STATEMENT OF INTEREST ACCRUAL

Year	Interest Accrued on FRDs (Rs in Crore)	2004-2005	100.05
2000-2001	0.99	2005-2006	115.01
2001-2002	14.11	2006-2007	165.77
2002-2003	31.93	2007-2008	270.01
2003-2004	93.07	Q1-2008	324.11
2004-2005	100.05	Q2-2008	375.53
2005-2006	115.01		
2006-2007	165.77		
2007-2008	270.01		
Q1-2008	324.11		
Q2-2008	375.53		

V ACTUAL INTEREST ACCRUAL

Year	Actual Interest Accrued on FRDs (Rs in Crore)	Difference between Interest Accrued shown in Balance Sheet and the Actual Status (Rs in Crore)
2000-2001	1.06	-0.06
2001-2002	0.38	13.73
2002-2003	0.71	31.22
2003-2004	1.81	91.26
2004-2005	0.51	99.54
2005-2006	4.71	110.30
2006-2007	2.04	163.73
2007-2008	1.00	269.01
Q1-2008	0.27	323.84
Q2-2008	0.07	375.46

VI FUDGED TDS DEDUCTION

Year	Tax Deducted at source as shown in The balance Sheet (Rs in Lakhs) (a)	Actual Tax Deducted at Source (Rs in Lakhs) (b)	Difference (Rs in Lakhs) (a-b)
2000-2001	20.59	23.17	– 2.58
2001-2002	8.55	8.05	0.50
2002-2003	519.62	15.28	504.34
2003-2004	1,903.02	23.26	1,879.76
2004-2005	2,090.28	10.12	2,080.16
2005-2006	2,594.00	106.10	2,487.90
2006-2007	3,710.00	45.85	3,664.15
2007-2008	6,104.00	19.76	6,084.24
Q1-2008	16,950.06	5.54	16,944.52
Q2-2008	3,050.00	1.53	3,048.47

VII Quarter-wise break-up raised in IMS through EXCEL Porting, entered and reconciled in Oracle Financials from 01.04.2003 to 31.12.2008 in Satyam Computers Service Limited.

Year (Period)	False Invoice Raised in Invoicing Management System (IMS)		False Invoices Entered in Oracle Financials		False Invoices Reconciled in Oracle Financials	
	No. of Invoices Raised	Invoice Amount in (Rs in Crore)	No. of Invoices entered	Invoice Amount in (Rs in Crore)	No. of Invoices for which receipt shown	Invoice Amount shown as received in (Rs in Crore)
Q1(Apr2003-Jun2003)	97	67.58	97	67.58	99	65.54
Q2(Jul 2003 – Sept 2003)	8	4.85	8	4.85	8	4.88
Q3 (Oct 2003 – Dec 2003)	50	40.25	50	40.25	49	39.83
Q4 (Jan2004 – Mar2004)	112	100.54	112	100.54	111	104.10
Total	267	213.21	267	213.21	267	214.35
Q1(Apr 2004 – Jun 2004)	112	86.38	111	86.37	111	89.12
Q2(Jul 2004 – Sept 2004)	64	41.50	63	40.71	62	39.17
Q3 (Oct 2004 – Dec 2004)	73	50.24	69	49.55	69	48.12
Q4 (Jan 2005 – Mar 2005)	217	142.40	208	132.81	208	128.85
Total	466	320.50	451	309.44	450	305.26

VII (*cont.*)

Year (Period)	False Invoice Raised in Invoicing Management System (IMS)		False Invoices Entered in Oracle Financials		False Invoices Reconciled in Oracle Financials	
	No. of Invoices Raised	Invoice Amount in (Rs in Crore)	No. of Invoices entered	Invoice Amount in (Rs in Crore)	No. of Invoices for which receipt shown	Invoice Amount shown as received in (Rs in Crore)
Q1(Apr 2005 – Jun 2005)	249	154.74	249	154.69	249	149.42
Q2(Jul 2005 – Sept 2005)	243	134.47	242	134.46	238	133.46
Q3 (Oct 2005 – Dec 2005)	296	163.48	291	150.17	262	141.44
Q4 (Jan 2006 – Mar 2006)	400	213.34	398	193.45	361	184.07
Total	1188	666.03	1180	632.78	1110	608.40
Q1(Apr 2006 – Jun 2006)	25	0.76	12	0.13	11	0.11
Q2(Jul 2006 – Sept 2006)	101	141.75	30	134.84	20	132.68
Q3 (Oct 2006 – Dec 2006)	385	283.95	237	242.34	237	227.37
Q4 (Jan 2007 – Mar 2007)	457	340.56	375	301.99	373	249.97
Total	968	767.01	654	679.30	641	610.14

VII (*cont.*)

Year (Period)	False Invoice Raised in Invoicing Management System (IMS)		False Invoices Entered in Oracle Financials		False Invoices Reconciled in Oracle Financials	
	No. of Invoices Raised	Invoice Amount in (Rs in Crore)	No. of Invoices entered	Invoice Amount in (Rs in Crore)	No. of Invoices for which receipt shown	Invoice Amount shown as received in (Rs in Crore)
Q1(Apr 2007 – Jun 2007)	680	394.20	473	322.62	473	289.08
Q2(Jul 2007 – Sept 2007)	741	415.13	486	320.56	485	277.25
Q3 (Oct 2007 – Dec 2007)	889	598.77	730	525.82	728	483.68
Q4 (Jan 2008 – Mar 2008)	794	565.30	794	565.30	794	540.13
Total	3104	1973.40	2483	1734.30	2480	1590.14
Q1(Apr 2008 – Jun 2008)	791	588.94	791	588.94	791	548.30
Q2(Jul 2008 – Sept 2008)	777	588.60	777	588.60	150	106.75
Total	1568	1177.54	1568	1177.54	941	655.06

VIII INFLATED ANNUAL SALES INCOME FIGURES

Period		Actual Sales in Crore (a)	Published and audited Sales in Crore (b)	Quantum of inflated Sales in Crore (b-a)	Percentage of inflated Sales (%)
2004-05	Q1	620.67	771.00	150.33	24
	Q2	815.04	848.10	33.06	4
	Q3	821.53	891.26	69.73	8
	Q4	789.94	953.34	163.40	21
Total		3047.18	3463.70	416.52	14
2005-06	Q1	904.48	1034.43	129.95	14
	Q2	972.75	1117.27	144.52	15
	Q3	1042.81	1222.63	179.82	17
	Q4	1077.63	1259.98	182.35	17
Total		3997.66	4634.31	636.65	16
2006-07	Q1	1330.90	1386.87	555.97	4
	Q2	1389.04	1537.70	148.66	11
	Q3	1368.30	1594.88	226.58	17
	Q4	1450.55	1709.03	258.48	18
Total		5538.80	6228.48	689.68	12
2007-08	Q1	1499.22	1759.08	259.86	17
	Q2	1605.58	1948.23	342.65	21
	Q3	1692.52	2110.59	418.07	25
	Q4	1798.25	2319.38	521.13	29
Total		6595.56	8137.28	1541.72	23
2008-09	Q1	2008.96	2526.90	517.94	26
	Q2	2246.24	2700.52	454.28	20
Grand Total		23434.39	27691.19	4256.80	18

IX Quarter-wise break up of non-existent debtors (Debt Amount) shown in Satyam Computers Balance Sheets

Period		Amount inflated in the Balance sheet (Rs in Crore.)
2003-04	Q1	2.00
	Q2	0.00
	Q3	0.41
	Q4	0.00
2004-05	Q1	0.00
	Q2	1.53
	Q3	1.43
	Q4	3.96
2005-06	Q1	5.26
	Q2	0.99
	Q3	8.73
	Q4	9.38
2006-07	Q1	0.01
	Q2	2.15
	Q3	14.96
	Q4	52.01
2007-08	Q1	333.54
	Q2	43.30
	Q3	42.13
	Q4	25.17
2008-09	Q1	40.63
	Q2	481.84

X The Satyam promoters and their individual income from the sale of shares

Sl. No.	Name of the promoter	Amount received on account of The sale of Satyam Computers Shares (Rs in Crore)
1	B Ramalinga Raju	26.68
2	B Rama Raju	26.68
3	B Suryanarayana Raju	181.17
4	B Pritam Teja	92.85
5	B Rama Raju Jr	92.54
6	Maytas Infrastructure Ltd.	190.16
7	B Satyanarayana Raju	22.99
8	B Appala Narasamma	17.58
9	B Jhansi Rani	56.39
Total		707.04

XI How the promoters' stakes in Satyam Computers were brought down

Year	No. of Shares held by Promoters (in lakhs)	% of Share held by promoters to the total share
June 1992	34.89	18.78
1993-94	34.89	18.78
1994-95	43.52	19.51
1995-96	51.56	19.82
October 1997	51.41	19.76
May 1998	51.90	19.95
May 1999	45.12	17.34
31.03.2000	74.30 (including Bonus Shares)	13.21
31.03.2000	74.30	13.21
31.03.2001	362.12(1:5 split)	12.88

XI (cont.)

Year	No. of Shares held by Promoters (in lakhs)	% of Share held by promoters to the total share
31.03.2002	361.12	11.48
31.03.2003	342.36	10.88
31.03.2004	327.46	10.35
31.03.2005	309.45	9.69
31.03.2006	278.68	8.59
31.03.2007	557.36 (including Bonus Shares)	8.35
31.03.2008	557.36	8.31
31.12.2008	126.14	1.87

XII Differences in the actual and published loading factors for offshore and onsite categories

Period	Offshore Category		Onsite Category	
	Investor link loading factor in %	Head count loading factor in %	Investor link link loading factor in %	Head count loading factor in %
Q2 FY 06-07	71.2	68.9	97.0	97.2
Q3 FY 06-07	68.5	63.8	96.8	97.4
Q4 FY 06-07	71.3	62.1	96.6	96.4
Q1 FY 07-08	76.5	63.8	96.2	96.5
Q2 FY 07-08	76.4	60.6	97.1	94.0
Q3FY 07-08	78.2	59.6	96.8	94.5
Q4 FY 07-08	81.8	58.5	97.3	93.4
Q1 FY 08-09	73.7	59.1	96.5	93.5
Q2 FY 08-09	76.1	61.8	96.1	94.1
Average	74.9	62.0	96.8	94.9

XIII Year and Quarter–wise Inflated Revenues and Operating Margins of Satyam Computers

Quarter-Year	Published Sales (Rs Cr.)	Actual Sales (Rs Cr.)	Expenditure (Rs Cr.)	Published Operating Margin (Rs Cr.)	Actual Operating Margin (Rs Cr.)
Q3-2007	1594.88	1352.54	1185.93	408.95	166.61
Q4-2007	1709.03	1407.05	1301.85	407.18	105.10
Q1-2008	1759.08	1436.47	1346.37	412.71	90.10
Q2-2008	1948.23	1627.28	1546.64	401.59	81.04
Q3-2008	2110.59	1584.77	1641.86	468.73	–57.09
Q4-2008	2319.38	1754.08	1773.89	545.49	–19.81
Q1-2009	2526.90	1937.96	1878.29	648.61	59.67
Q2-2009	2700.52	2111.93	2051.25	649.27	60.68

Glossary

AS: Compliance of Accounting Standards in the preparation and presentation of financial statements is mostly mandatory. Most countries have national advisory committee on accounting standards. Government and regulatory authorities often work together to set these standards.

Audit Committee: Comprises mostly independent directors of a company to liaise between the board of directors and external auditors of the company.

Basel Accords: Refers to periodical recommendations – such as Basel I, Basel II and Basel III – on banking supervision (laws and regulations) by a committee of central bankers and regulatory authorities principally from G-20 countries.

Bookcooking: Coined by the author to mean cooked-up books of accounts or falsified record of business transactions.

Bookkeeping: Keeping record of business transactions. A bookkeeper is an accounting person who keeps record of an organisation's day-to-day transactions, including sales, purchases, incomes and payments.

Bottom Line: The ultimate result of a company's annual profit and loss account showing net profit or net loss.

CAG: The Comptroller and Auditor General of India is a Constitutional authority and the apex statutory auditor of government accounts, covering a wide range of areas such as union and state governments and public sector business and industrial undertakings.

CBI: The Central Bureau of Investigation is India's biggest crime investigation agency working under the union government with a quasi judicial power.

Certified Public Accountant: A qualified professional accountant with a public practice licence to audit books of accounts of an organisation or a body corporate.

Chaebol: Signifies a large South Korean family-controlled business organisation with global reach.

Chartered Accountant: A member of the Institute of Chartered Accountants of India (ICAI) or of a similar organisation in a country.

Corporate Governance: A code of corporate management conduct with regard to financial disclosures for the knowledge and benefit of stakeholders.

Dai-Ichi Kangyo bank: A powerful post-war Japanese financial institution creating the country's largest loosely interlocked financial-industrial conglomerate (Keiretsu) which merged with Fuji Bank and Industrial Bank of Japan to form Mizuho Financial Group in 2000.

Derivatives: According to the International Financial Reporting Standards (IFRS), a derivative is a financial instrument whose value changes in response to specific index. A derivative requires little net investment and is settled at a future date. The US GAAP and IFRS specify rules for the recognition and measurement of derivatives, options and forward agreements.

Dodd-Frank Act: A federal statute in the US signed into law in 2010, following the collapse of several Wall Street banks and mutual funds, to usher in further reform of banking and financial regulations to ensure better consumer protection.

External Audit: Involves a periodical examination or review of any legal entity or organisation's books of accounts and financial statements conducted by independent auditors or third-party auditors appointed for the purpose by members or ordinary shareholders of the entity for the latter's knowledge and understanding. The profession is regulated.

GAAP: It refers to the primary consideration in the selection of accounting policies by an entity as being that the financial statements prepared and presented on the basis of such policies present a 'true and fair' view of the state of affairs of that entity as at the balance sheet date. The Generally Accepted Accounting Principles may vary from country to country as in the cases of US GAAP, UK GAAP and Indian GAAP.

Hawala: It refers mostly to a system of money swap for the purpose of money laundering. Money owed by a debtor to a creditor is paid by a person who owes the debtor money. Hawala transactions are usually based on trust without keeping a written record.

ICAI: The Institute of Chartered Accountants of India, self-regulatory body of its members and professional accountants, set up under an act of Parliament called Chartered Accountants Act, 1949. It operates through various technical committees and issues guidance notes on various matters related to accountancy and auditing.

Internal Audit: It is conducted by a legal entity or organisation for measuring its accounting policies and procedures through a group of experts or professionals employed by the entity for the purpose and seek its advice, if and when necessary. The profession of internal auditors is unregulated.

Keidanren: A post World War II Japanese association of big business organisations set up to mediate differences between member industries and advise the government on economic policies. It is one of Japan's most powerful organisations.

Off-Balance-Sheet: A business transaction or financials normally not mentioned in an organisation's balance sheet. It mostly concerns uncertain assets and liabilities subject to management judgement or, maybe, legal judgement. Some organisations may report such assets and liabilities in the balance sheet as 'assets under management'. Off-balance-sheet items are very often tricky and controversial.

PAC: The Public Accounts Committee is a parliamentary accounting oversight body to prevent leakage or misuse of public funds and conducts independent investigation based on CAG reports.

RBI: The Reserve Bank of India is the country's central bank and the regulatory authority for the banking and financial sector, including non-banking financial companies.

Sarbanes-Oxley Act: Enacted in 2002 as a public company accounting reform and investor protection law following the financial collapse of a series of giant US corporations.

SEBI: The Securities and Exchange Board of India, set up in 1992 to bring about a major securities market reform, is a regulatory agency to protect the interests of investors in securities and help develop a healthy securities market. It is the capital markets watchdog.

SEC: A federal US agency – Securities and Exchange Commission – set up under Securities Act, 1933 to regulate the securities industry and stock exchanges. It enforces and administers the federal securities laws, subject to oversight of the US Congress, to protect investors and ensures compliance with annual reporting requirements.

Stock Option: A non-cash compensation given by companies to employees and senior management personnel as an incentive to better performance leading to higher stock price appreciation. Employees given stock option benefit stand to gain directly when share price goes up. Stock options can also be offered to a company's non-employees such as independent directors, consultants, lawyers and promoters for services rendered.

Window Dressing: An account deliberately dressed up to project a favourable financial picture of a company rather than the factual position of its affairs.

Index